Looking For Eric

Written by Paul Laverty
Directed by Ken Loach

route

First published in 2009 by Route
PO Box 167, Pontefract, WF8 4WW
info@route-online.com
www.route-online.com

In association with Sixteen Films
2nd Floor, 187 Wardour Street, London, W1F 8ZB

ISBN (13): 978-1-901927-41-2
ISBN (10): 1-901927-41-5

Cover design:
GOLDEN www.wearegolden.co.uk
from artwork supplied by Icon Film Distribution

Route support:
Ian Daley, Isabel Galán, Eimhear McMahon,
Peter Maguire, Tony Maguire, Rebecca O'Brien, Emma Smith

A catalogue for this book is available from the British Library

Printed in the UK by CPI Bookmarque, Croydon, CR0 4TD

Route is supported by Arts Council England

Contents

It all began with a beautiful pass from Eric Cantona...

Paul Laverty
Writer
Introduction

When Ken first told me that Eric Cantona wanted to meet him I wasn't sure if it was another of his wind-ups. I knew he had been suffering; his beloved team Bath City had been in trouble and I thought he might have been fantasising again. But there Eric was…the King himself, sitting in our offices.

We met to discuss a short treatment Eric and his brothers had prepared for French film company Why Not about a real fan who had followed Eric from Leeds United to Manchester United and as a result lost his job, his mates and his family. I think it had strong possibilities, but in the end a fictional story, and the freedom therein, has its own enormous pull.

Maybe it was the terrible flu I had when we met that day, but as we talked my mind kept drifting off to many of those wonderful goals Eric scored, his flashes of inspiration, his temper, the infamous karate kick, the 'Sardine' press conference, the songs of the crowd, and for no good reason other than it stuck in my mind, that absolute peach of a goal he scored against Sunderland. But it was crystal clear to both Ken and myself that Eric's intriguing character both on the field and off opened up fascinating possibilities.

After having recently completed two tough films (*It's A Free World* and *The Wind That Shakes the Barley*) Ken, Rebecca (Producer) and myself had a firm inclination that no matter what our next project would be, there would have to be a strong element of mischief in it to keep us sane.

For quite some time too I had been talking to Ken about a possible story involving grandparents. I knew this wasn't going to get financiers salivating but since my own kids were born I have become more and more curious about the complex interweaving and multifaceted roles grandparents have in our lives. In many ways they keep the world turning, but with few exceptions, they are invisible on screen, or grossly stereotyped.

Older protagonists open up an incredible well of past lives, so I have always been intrigued by the possibility of a story that would look just as much to the past as unfold in the present. Our past isn't gone, but is fiercely loaded.

A cluster of questions and contradictory notions kept coming to mind in one big unmanageable tangle. I found myself wondering how we define turning points in our lives; how people we have met along the way have left an indelible impression on our souls and whom we will probably recall on our deathbeds; I wondered about accidents of timing, of when couples meet and who they are at that moment. Past mistakes may fester; hurt and blame can tumble over each other in a endless cycle that can still cast a shadow on our present. I thought about our fantastic gift of memory that can make thirty years ago burn with the intensity of yesterday. I reflected on how we can get 'stuck', what makes for change, and what a complex endeavour it is to understand each other. What is hidden, and what is just too painful to confront? I wondered about our capacity to forgive, not just the other, but ourselves.

And as we grow older, what happens to our confidence and that fragile sense of ourselves? What we become seldom matches what we might have imagined in those fearless days of our early twenties. A long life can be a right bloody mess and it is a never-ending challenge to manage all the new layers, which are in a constant state of flux. Sometimes it is a closer call than we dare admit to slide from moments of crisis over to breakdown and possible madness.

Maybe some of the above fermented with the flu, my conversations with Ken, and the unexpected – Eric's goal against Sunderland. It is no ordinary strike, but a moment of beauty; his physical prowess, the dribble around two defenders, his sublime one-two with teammate Brian McClair – and all the while you can sense the excitement of the crowd swell – and then the final audacious flash of imagination to chip and swerve the ball in a beautiful arc to land a few inches inside the left-hand post. The crowd roared with pleasure and amazement. No wonder Eduardo Galeano calls a goal football's orgasm. But it wasn't the orgasm that got me, it was Eric's pose after he struck. He sticks out his chest, honours all those present with a full circle as if looking every single one of the 50,000 fans in the eye, and saying, 'My gift to you'! It was a moment of supreme self-confidence, man and stadium in communion.

For no good reason I caught an imaginary glimpse of a man called Eric Bishop on the terraces that day. That goal kept him going for months as he struggled through his chaotic life. When we join Little Eric, father, stepfather, grandfather, and at least twice separated, the Cantona days of going to the football with his mates are long gone. Unlike Big Eric, he senses people see through him. He not only feels he is losing control of everything around him, but much more terrifying he feels he can't even rely on himself. When Little Eric looks himself in the eye he confronts a lost man, heading for the precipice. I daydreamed about the possibilities of throwing these two Erics

11

together to see what would happen – and what freer place to meet than in the mind of Eric Bishop as he struggled to keep his sanity, ambushed by both the past and the present, and hiding away from the world in his little bedroom. Could Eric Bishop find himself again?

Ken and I entertained ourselves with many possibilities but it was all in the abstract until we met again with Eric to discuss this rather strange juxtaposition. Did Big Eric fancy being a figment of a mentally unstable grandfather's imagination... how would he like to be a nonconformist shrink smoking spliffs...and could he dance rock and roll? At least I knew he would love the proverbs.

In all honesty as I made my way to Paris to meet Eric again I had no idea how this would all turn out. The first thing was to see if Eric was open to this madness, and secondly, to get some sense of the man. It turned out to be a fantastic few days with Eric laughing out loud at some of the daft scenes we had imagined and he suggested many more. From the outset he was remarkably modest, and best of all, he was prepared to laugh at himself. It was important for me too that he genuinely had some empathy for the fictional Eric and his life. This gave me a tremendous sense of freedom when I came to write the script.

Eric passed on a few gems over those days. And perhaps befitting the man, he often turned expectation on its head. I asked him what it felt like to have 50,000 people chanting his name and singing songs about him. He told me it was scary; he was scared it might stop. (It reminded me of Maradona: 'I need them to need me.') He told me he set out to surprise the crowd every game he played, but to do that, he had to surprise himself first. I asked him about his greatest football moment ever, fully expecting a winning goal in a cup final or league decider. He surprised again, telling me it was a pass he made to Ryan Giggs. (We couldn't find footage of this pass and subsequent goal but his pass to Irwin, which we use in the film, was ingrained in my memory.) But what if Giggs had missed? Eric's reply: 'You must trust your teammates. Always.' This fitted in perfectly with what I imagined would be a key idea in the film, of Little Eric finding the courage to take a risk, and trust his mates and Lily again, with his own fragility.

I asked him about his nine-month ban, a horrendous length of time when you consider how short the career of a professional footballer is. After such an ordered, disciplined life, the routine of the weekly fixtures, to say nothing of the adrenaline-high of playing in front of a packed stadium, I asked him how he managed to confront the solitude of it all. He told me he had to find something to fill him up. 'What?' I asked. He replied, 'I tried to play the trumpet.' How about that…this footballing genius in front of a worshipping crowd one week, and the next, in the loneliness of his room, all fingers and thumbs struggling with a trumpet.

In one fell swoop celebrity culture punctured; no matter who we are, Big Eric or Little Eric, here we are battling to make sense of each day. I love that surreal scene in the film when Big Eric armed with his trumpet, and Little Eric armed with his memory, stand on a council flat balcony and look out over Manchester and the world beyond. I find each misplaced note magical, a hymn to all those imperfect messy lives out there, a celebration of our fragility, and a clarion call to make that leap of faith to confide in those that love you. Always.

Ken Loach
Director

I got a message that Eric Cantona was trying to get in touch...

It was about two or three years ago. Without him there would be no film. A very nice French producer, Pascal Caucheteux, spoke with Rebecca [O'Brien, Producer] and suggested that he and Eric and we meet. Obviously we knew Eric Cantona, knew his public persona very well, and knew him as a fantastic footballer. And they knew that Paul [Laverty, Writer] and I were interested in football. So we met. Eric had a few ideas that were all very interesting, in particular a story of his relationship with one fan. Paul and I couldn't really make that work in terms of narrative and characters and development, but we thought it was an interesting area to explore – not only the enjoyment of football and the part that football plays in people's lives, but also the notion of celebrity and how celebrities are built up in the press and on television: they have a superhuman quality in people's minds.

Paul went away with a blank sheet of paper and wrote a story that tried to bring in all these elements. There were no major misgivings about showing it to Eric because we'd met two or three times and we had a good sense of who he was: he just seemed somebody who was not reverent about himself and had a twinkle in his eye about the whole project. It was fun, rather than some heavy-handed affair. We were just hoping he would enjoy it and he was kind enough to say that he did.

Why Cantona?

He's original and bright and sharp and perceptive. He thinks a little outside the game and his jousts with journalists were always funny and witty. He's obviously a man of some substance – we knew that about him just from the way he'd been in public, from both before the seagulls quote and afterwards. As we talked to him – particularly as Paul talked to him – his thoughts on the game and on his place in it and what he tried to do and how he approached it all became part of the project.

When Eric walks in a room you really know he's there. It's true of very few people but he's a man with considerable charisma and magnetism. Actors talk about natural projection, in that you can communicate from the stage to the back of the auditorium without apparently doing anything. Eric did that on a football field – he communicated to 50,000 people. That's an extraordinary natural ability.

In Manchester he was treated with reverence and affection. We had to keep him under wraps a bit – it's the first time I've ever had paparazzi lurking round a set. And if you were with him in the street the traffic would slow down and people would seize him by the hand.

I went to a game with him at Old Trafford. Even without knowing he was there they were singing the Cantona songs – they were singing his name when he hadn't been there for a decade. Then when they discovered he was there the roof went up. Grown men wept! As we were leaving old fellas were coming up to him shaking him by the hand. Very few players have inspired such affection.

Why Football?

I only know it as a spectator but to go to a game is very social: you meet the same, quite large group of people and what you have in common is support for the team. It's nothing to do with work, it's nothing to do with anything except the game and that wide selection of disparate people.

But the game itself is like a gymnasium for your emotions. You experience everything. Hope, joy, sorrow, grief, suspense, anguish. Delirious ecstasy when the goal goes in. It's all those things but they're all contained in a safe framework that – I can't say, 'it doesn't matter' – but in the end it is only a game and real life carries on. It's a huge therapeutic exercise where you have all these emotions but nevertheless they're within a safe environment.

Who is Eric Bishop, your lead character?

He's an intelligent man who suffers from panic attacks and it's really interfered with his ability to stay in a relationship. His response to it is just to put his head in the sand, go out with the lads, go to the games, have a drink and not deal with it. The consequence is his first marriage broke down. He then married someone else who developed a drink problem. She had two sons by different fathers. When she finally went off the rails he was left with these two lads and because at heart he's a very generous person, when they were younger he did have a reasonable relationship with them. But as they've become teenagers they do what teenagers do, which is if they see a weakness they exploit it. They destroy him. He's left with a big house that he can't manage, and of course chaos breeds chaos. He can barely hold his job together and when we first see him he's in the middle of a panic attack.

How was the film cast?

Next to the script the casting is the most important thing. I worked with Kahleen [Crawford, Casting Director] again and we saw unknown actors, well-known actors, everybody – we just try to be as inclusive as possible. It's always important that the film is rooted somewhere specific, so we did restrict it to people from Manchester or nearby. The Eric in the film is a Manchester United supporter when most Manchester United supporters came from Manchester. So we thought it was important that he was played by a Manchester man. With Steve Evets we were able to sense that he was a man on the edge. He's also funny but not in a way that he's playing comedy: he's just being true. We look for true responses and then when somebody reveals themself, that they reveal themself in a way that is in line with the character. Because you can get somebody who's really brilliant – right social class, everything right – but as they reveal themself in their performance it's something different to the character. You've got to find somebody who's good in all those ways but also true to the character you want on the screen.

How was Cantona himself introduced in to the action?

There was a moment! It was very elaborate. Surprise is the hardest thing to act, and Steve [Evets] had no idea – he knew that Eric Cantona was involved as a producer but he didn't know that he was in the film. On the day he was going to be in it we brought him in to the house and in to the bedroom. I said to Steve, 'The light's not quite right. We're going to have to put up a bit of black to minimise the reflection. Give us ten minutes.' Steve went out for a smoke, Eric Cantona hid behind a black drape that we'd put round the camera and then we played the scene. Steve was looking towards the life-size Cantona poster and Eric slipped out and stood behind him, and spoke. Unfortunately we had some Belgian camera assistants and when Steve heard the voice he thought it was one of them speaking. So he stood there and he didn't know what to do. The first take it didn't quite work. But there was still surprise enough for the second take.

Tonally, how do you go from comic scenes to more serious moments?
You can only be truthful. And that again is down to finding people who can be truthful and naturally funny. Or truthful and naturally touching. The moment there's a sense of, 'Now it's a comedy scene,' and 'Now it's a sad scene,' it wouldn't work. That's why somebody like John [Henshaw] is a good actor. He's serious and he's funny without a change of step. Ricky Tomlinson is like that as well. He can be funny and in exactly the same mood he can be serious. That he doesn't have to change gear is the essential thing.

What do you hope an audience will take from the film?
Just the fact that it's about friendship and about coming to terms with who you are. It's a film against individualism: we're stronger as a gang than we are on our own. You can be pretentious about this but it is about the solidarity of friends, which is epitomised in a crowd of football supporters. But also where you work and the people you work alongside. Although that seems an almost trite observation, it's still not the spirit of the age. Or it hasn't been the spirit of the age for the last thirty years, where people are your competitors, not your comrades.

21

Cantona plays the trumpet in the film. Does he have a future as a musician?

When George Fenton recorded the music and heard Eric playing, I sent Eric a text saying, 'The musicians are impressed but suggest you don't give up the football just yet.' He texted back and said, 'Maybe they think I take their work.'

Eric Cantona
Lui-même

When I met with the French co-producers [Pascal Caucheteux and Vincent Maraval], we all said that a story about my relationship with the fans needed an English director. The relationship with the fans in England is very special. The director had to be a football fan to understand, somebody who had experienced this kind of feeling. The first name was Ken Loach. We were a bit crazy to think about it but we thought we would give it a try – we said the worst thing that can happen is he says no.

We met him with Rebecca [O'Brien, Producer] and Paul [Laverty, Writer] and they said, yeah, maybe it's a good idea. We will try to develop and write it but we don't promise anything. If after a few weeks we feel that we cannot do it... They were being very, very honest. And they found a way with Paul to write a great script. We received it and read it and we loved it – we have been very, very lucky.

Paul and I had spent an afternoon talking about the games, football, everything. All of the proverbs are from him. They made me laugh a lot when I read them – and I think perhaps he laughed a lot also when he wrote them! I didn't mind saying them at all – no, no – I loved it.

The goals were chosen by them, but I agree with the choice. I think it's a good balance – some goals from twenty or thirty yards, some goals with chips, some headers – different types of goals. There were maybe some better goals – for instance, the goal scored against Arsenal when we won at home 5-0. It was a beautiful goal and it is not in the movie. Some are not so nice, but you have also to find a rhythm and a balance.

It was nice to be back in Manchester. I love the people there. That never fades, or not from my side, no. It seems to be always the same. It is strange, of course, when you stop playing football. But I have been lucky to have other passions like acting. And the trumpet, yes, like you see in the film – but I'm having to practice a lot.

In the film I am Eric Cantona in Eric Bishop's mind, in his imagination. That's the way he sees me. That gives me a lot of distance from myself – how do you say, *auto-dérision*? [self-deprecating humour] – so I liked it a lot.

I have worked in other movies and there I can hide behind the character. In this one I have to be myself. It was a strange feeling. I asked Ken questions that I have never asked before because in the days before the shooting I didn't feel very comfortable and I need to be comfortable with the character. It was a good experience – something special. It's like being... and watching yourself being. You have to find spontaneity, be yourself, but in a fiction. It was a strange exercise but very interesting.

If I play the relationship between a fan and myself very seriously I think it is a bit pretentious, arrogant, and not very interesting. Ken has a very light touch – not in the wrong sense, but he can make things funny and also real. So in this film there is a lot of humour, a lot of sensibility, emotion... auto-dérision!

Me, I was very proud of how the film showed the feeling I

had with the fans, the way I saw the fans, the way I received the energy of the fans. That is all there in this movie. It's unusual to capture that – they are nice people, nice, beautiful people, always a lot of solidarity, a lot of friendship. I was moved by their energy. I love this kind of thing because these days it's unusual, solidarity, friendship. In the film we can see that on the inside they are beautiful people.

Eric Bishop, the love story, the relationship he had with his kids, the misunderstanding he has with his wife twenty years before…sometimes we don't want to say things and we break relationships because we don't speak enough. It's why I appear in his life – to encourage him to speak. Or if he can't speak, write – but communicate. If you cannot be together you cannot be together, but you must say things. That is very important and this film speaks about that also.

Looking For Eric
Screenplay

1. ROAD IN A MANCHESTER SUBURB

Wheels screech around corners. ERIC BISHOP [fifty-two years of age but much older inside] drives erratically. He wears a postman's uniform, its jacket open to reveal a faded shirt with buttons done up irregularly, leaving his collar massively skewed. His hair is too long and straggly, he has five days' growth over pasty white skin, but it is his sunken eyes that are most disturbing.

In his mind he hears his daughter's voice:

> VOICE OVER
> [Cheery] Dad…I want to ask you a big big
> favour…a big big favour…[same voice, change
> of tone]…you really let me down Dad…really
> let me down…[man's voice, sarcastic challenge]
> Now we'll see what you're made of…

ANOTHER PART OF THE ROAD:

Eric's eyes are fixed on the road. He overtakes on a dangerous bend.

ROUNDABOUT – OUTSKIRTS OF THE CITY:

Eric approaches a medium roundabout.

Fatal mistake, and instant chaos – he goes round the wrong way against the traffic.

Cars screech and swerve as Eric, frozen in his seat, hugs the inside lane.

FROM ERIC'S POV: on the edge of his consciousness there is a dim awareness of strange noises – horns, sirens, and screeching tyres – the world is a distant surreal blur. Around and around he goes, totally stuck in his circular track.

CUT TO BLACK: TITLES

The titles, white on black, are accompanied by a soundtrack of more horns and sirens. There are glimpses of the following scenes:

Two police bikes screech to a halt and try to block off more traffic entering the roundabout.

Another officer on foot is already trying to wave Eric down. He stands in front of him but has to dive for cover as Eric drives on.

                    OFFICER
        Wanker!

Another officer is on his radio.

                OFFICER (CONT'D)
        Won't believe this…got some mad bastard on
        the roundabout going round the wrong way!

                      HQ
        Maybe he's French?

                    OFFICER
        No excuse…Send an ambulance…and a
        shrink.

Round and around Eric goes.

32

INSIDE THE ESCORT:

Eric grips the steering wheel too tightly.

> VOICE OVER
> Dad...I want to ask you a big big favour...[as
> if voice is stuck too] a big big favour...a big
> big favour...a big big favour...a big big
> favour...[man's voice] Now we'll see what
> you're made of...now we'll see what your
> made of...[change of voice again, cheery]
> Dad...I want to ask you a big big favour...

The traffic is cut and Eric circles alone.

> VOICE OVER (CONT'D)
> [Man's voice again] Now we'll see what you're
> made of...

A powerful police car with flashing lights runs parallel to him.

An incredulous police officer in the passenger seat of his vehicle holding a megaphone has his window wound down and blasts him orders to stop.

> OFFICER
> Stop the car!...We are ordering you to pull
> over now...Stop the car now Sir!! Can you
> hear me Sir? You ya bloody clown...Pull over!

FROM ERIC'S POV: an angry face shouting at him but it doesn't register.

INSIDE POLICE CAR:

> OFFICER (CONT'D)
> [To police driver] Not drunk...just off his
> fucking trolley...

DRIVER

Jesus…this could go on for hours…

OFFICER

How many miles to a gallon in an old Ford
Escort?

They stare across at Eric and notice his shoulders shake.

OFFICER (CONT'D)

Shit…I think he's crying…

Both Eric and police car keep going round and round and
round…

2. PSYCHIATRIC UNIT – NIGHT

Eric, in bed, [perhaps one of six] stares around him. It is the
middle of the night. Several of the other patients do not look in
the best of shape and perhaps one is strapped to a bed. Some
deeply disturbed faces. Eric notices.

Eric is frightened and vulnerable, but is now fully aware of his
circumstances. He spots a nurse.

ERIC

What time is it please?

A male nurse approaches.

NURSE

Five in the morning…try and sleep…

ERIC

I'm so sorry about all the fuss…really really
sorry…don't know what got into me…

                        NURSE

You were very very lucky nobody was hurt…

                        ERIC

I've got an early shift…can you get me my
clothes?

                        NURSE

You can't leave just now…a doctor will see you
in the morning…

                        ERIC

I can't be late…

                        NURSE

Rest now…relax.

The nurse leaves.

Eric closes his eyes and tries to breathe deeply to calm himself.

                        ERIC

        Oh Lily…

He begins to weep into his pillow and covers his face in
embarrassment. Deep painful sobs.

                    ERIC (CONT'D)

        Ah Lil…

3. FLASHBACK – SHOPPING PRECINCT – DAY BEFORE

Eric [dressed as he was earlier in scene 1 with uniform on]
peeks from behind a pillar. He stares at an attractive woman
[LILY, fifty-one years old] who gently pushes a pram back and
forward. She is simply dressed but in very good taste;
imaginative, but not too flashy. She has obviously taken great

care of herself. She has great posture and exudes a sense of vitality. She is intelligent and confident.

She checks her watch and then stares around her. Eric ducks behind the pillar for a moment before sneaking a look at her once more.

Eric stares at her as she stoops into the pram and talks in gentle tones to a baby. She laughs spontaneously at the child; something beautiful and simple between infant and grandmother for a few short moments.

Eric can't bear it. He ducks back again and leans against the pillar.

After a moment he marches off in the opposite direction without looking back.

BACK TO PSYCHIATRIC UNIT – NIGHT:

Eric is still fretful and mumbles to himself.

ERIC (CONT'D)

    Lily…Lily…

4. CORRIDOR TO PSYCHIATRIC UNIT – MORNING

An enormous bear of a man [late forties/early fifties] strides along the corridor in a postman's uniform. [He is a force of nature, with boundless energy. He exudes warmth, but a sense of danger too. Despite much of the muscle from his early days of weight-lifting having turned to fat he displays the easy confidence and natural leadership of someone with great physical presence.]

He steams through double swing doors, which crash behind him.

He enters the psychiatric unit which has windows looking on the ward where Eric slept.

Eric is in the process of dressing and thanking a nurse by the bed.

A young psychiatrist tentatively greets the postman.

PSYCHIATRIST
Are you Mr [pause] Meatballs?

MEATBALLS
[Deep gravelly voice] My nickname...we spoke.

PSYCHIATRIST
Yes...he said we should phone you...

Eric and Meatballs catch sight of each other through the glass. Eric gives him an embarrassed wave.

MEATBALLS
Can't believe it...my best mate...sanest man I know...chess champion...works like a dog...Is he cracking up?

The young doctor is slightly taken aback by his energy and directness.

PSYCHIATRIST
A little 'sticky' patch...more common than you think. He's fully aware of what happened and is very embarrassed...feeling vulnerable...run down...

MEATBALLS
Run down...too right he's run down...by a pair of stepson wankers who should have been strangled at birth! What's wrong with him?

PSYCHIATRIST
A little trouble with his self confidence.
Happens to the best of us...

Inside Eric looks massively embarrassed and apologetic. He shakes hands with a nurse and thanks her warmly.

MEATBALLS
[Staring at his mate] We'll sort him out...don't you worry...

The psychiatrist hands him a letter.

PSYCHIATRIST
A community psychiatric nurse will be in touch...give him this...through his GP we'll make a referral. He really needs to see someone he can talk to...

5. MEATBALLS' VAN

Meatballs drives his van with the occasional look at Eric.

Silence for some time.

MEATBALLS
How are you Eric?

ERIC
Great.

MEATBALLS
How are you feeling?

ERIC
Fantastic.

Silence.

MEATBALLS

Guinness Book of Records eh?

Eric glances at him.

MEATBALLS (CONT'D)

Three thousand times round the same
roundabout...Don't tell me...a career
change...postman to astronaut?

ERIC

I was daydreaming...

MEATBALLS

You were going round the wrong way! A
miracle nobody was killed...what's going on?

Eric shakes his head in embarrassment.

Silence again.

MEATBALLS (CONT'D)

Eric...do you want to talk about it?

ERIC

Shit! Who do you think I am? A good night's
kip and I'll feel as fit as a butcher's dog.
[Pause] Where's my car?

MEATBALLS

Fucked. You can use my old banger till you
win the pools...but you're not getting the
bloody keys till I know you are okay...

ERIC

What about the police?

MEATBALLS

I asked…they'll do a report but unlikely to do
anything given your 'psychological condition'.

Meatballs hands him the letter given to him by the psychiatrist.

MEATBALLS (CONT'D)

A referral…

Eric takes it. He crumples it up and sticks it in his pocket.

MEATBALLS (CONT'D)

I was your best man…if you can't speak to me
who can you speak to?

ERIC

Does anyone know?

Meatballs is slightly embarrassed.

MEATBALLS

I told a few of the boys. I was worried sick…

ERIC

Fucking big mouth! I'm feeling great!

MEATBALLS

You got to trust your mates Eric…who else
have you got?

6. ERIC'S HOUSE

Meatballs drops Eric outside a badly run down Victorian three-storey house.

MEATBALLS

Eric…if you need anything…no matter
what…give me a call…anytime. I mean it.

Eric glances at his mate and nods.

The little garden outside the front door is covered in junk. [Half cannibalised mopeds, bikes and miscellaneous bits and pieces.]

Eric trudges his way inside as two dodgy teenagers pass him by on the way out.

> TEENAGER 1
> Left the gear inside…van will be here in an
> hour or two…tell Ryan.

> ERIC
> No more of your shit in here…

> TEENAGER 2
> Cool it…A few hours man…

> ERIC
> How did you get in?

The boys catch each other's eye, a hint of a smirk on their faces, and they are off again.

Eric enters the hall. He stares at two enormous heavy duty pneumatic drills splattered in mud [for digging up roads] leaning up against a wall.

Inside there are the sounds of TVs.

A scruffy teenager, RYAN [nineteen years old] still half asleep, dressed only in his pants, wanders downstairs.

> ERIC
> Did you give those guys a key?

Ryan ignores him and goes into the kitchen to raid the fridge. Eric goes into the front room. It looks like a refugee camp. A

TV blares in the corner. Eric steps over the mess of dirty dishes, cans, and DVD cases to switch it off.

He moves down into the kitchen. He surveys the bombsite of dirty dishes spreading from sink to bench to kitchen table. Dirty clothes pile up and overwhelm a linen basket. Another TV without an audience. He switches it off too and goes upstairs.

A very attractive seventeen-year-old girl barely dressed in the skimpiest of nightdresses appears from the bathroom. She is taken aback for a moment when she notices Eric on the stairs.

                    GIRL
        Who are you?

                    ERIC
        I live here.

                    GIRL
        Ah...Ryan's stepdad...hello.

She skips into Ryan's room and closes the door. Still the sound of other TVs.

As he passes Ryan's room Eric can hear the sound of the girl's laugh above the TV. He pokes his head around the door.

                    ERIC
        I want that shit out of the house...

Ryan and the girl are sharing a spliff. Ryan blows smoke rings.

Eric turns away and climbs the stairs to another bedroom on the top floor. Another bombsite. A sleeping sixteen-year-old teenager, JESS, is spreadeagled out.

ERIC

Jess…get up. It's 12 o'clock…you're late for
school.

Jess rolls over to face the wall. Eric whips the blankets from
him, but Jess curls up tighter and pulls the pillow up over his
head.

Eric moves towards the window to open it, but trips up over a
bundle of clothes and blankets on the floor. First one sleepy face
and then another peer from below him.

BOY 1

Watch your big feet man…just stood on my
leg…

ERIC

Pardon fucking me!

Eric grabs a loose pillow and before he knows it he is pounding
the two boys on the floor in a rage. He totally loses it.

The boys take cover from the pillow and shout out.

BOY 2

Leave off you mad bastard…

JESS

Eric! What the fuck are you doing?!

Eric swings round and attacks Jess with the pillow. The two
boys can't help but snigger as Jess retreats on the bed under the
blows from an unhinged Eric.

ERIC

How many fucking times have I told
you?!…Eh! [as he pounds]…This isn't a
fucking youth hostel!…A doss house! A refugee

camp!…Does anyone listen to me in my own home?

JESS

Calm down Eric…

ERIC

I'm fucking sick of you all!!

The pillow bursts and feathers start flying all around. The two boys on the floor are spellbound – caught between fear and laughter. They duck under the covers again as Eric takes a last swing at them from the now pathetic pillow fast losing its plumage. The pillow disintegrates in Eric's hand and he tosses it down.

He marches from the room. The three boys stare at each other in amazement.

BOY 2

Fucking hell…

Eric, puffed out from his exertions, opens the door to his sanctuary, which is like an independent bedsit.

The entire room is taken up with memorabilia from Manchester United. There are old photographs from the sixties all the way through to the present.

But pride of place goes to a full-size cut-out cardboard figure of Eric Cantona in his prime. His barrel chest sticks out, his shirt collar is up, and he stares out at the world as if he owns the place.

The phone rings in his room but he doesn't answer. The answering machine clicks on. It is the same woman's voice from before.

VOICE

> Dad…me again. Where the hell are you?! Will
> you phone me…is your mobile working? I'm
> going to miss two classes now…got to rush
> back to pick up Daisy. Mum waited on you for
> over an hour…For God's sake Dad if you
> couldn't make it why didn't you call?…[Pause]
> You really let me down Dad…I'm so pissed
> off…

Eric collapses onto a seat. He tries to catch his breath.

He looks crushed and ashamed of himself.

Eventually he looks up at the Cantona poster for a few moments.

ERIC

> Ever had a shrink Eric? Know what he asked
> me?…[Long pause] When was the last time you
> were happy?

Silence for a few moments as Eric stares into space.

Eric closes his eyes and sinks into the chair.

7. FLASHBACK – FOOTBALL MAGIC

The swelling intoxicating roar of an expectant crowd from over ten years ago overwhelms Eric Bishop…

Miscellaneous scenes of brilliance from Eric Cantona. [Every goal Cantona ever scored is ingrained in Eric's mind.]

Right foot, left foot, stunning headers, free kicks, dribbling…

COMMENTATOR'S VOICE
That man again...Eric Cantona!

Delightful and imaginative passes that split defences...

Cantona now in slow motion...just walking on the pitch with an Andy Gray type over-the-top commentary over in the background.

COMMENTATOR
'Flawed' genius?...How dare they? 100%
genius if you ask me...Look at the way he
sticks out that chest...pulls up that collar...the
man oozes talent and self-belief. Look at that
for Gallic pride and supreme confidence...he'd
terrify the best defence in the world. No
wonder the fans call him God!

8. FLASHBACK – SUPPORTERS' BUS – 1995

Manchester supporters' bus on way home after a terrific away victory. A trimmer Eric Bishop and his mates [passing round the drinks] are in full voice, singing what seems like a corny hymn.

SUPPORTERS
What a friend we have in Jesus, he's our
Saviour from afar, what a friend we have in
Jesus, and his name is Cantona...

Eric's daughter SAM [fifteen years old] blasts it out too.

Meatballs stands in the corridor of the bus and is chief conductor of the chaos, while the more effervescent SPLEEN punches the air too as their hero's name [the tune now transforms into the Marseillaise] reaches the climax...

VOICES

Cantonaaaa…Cantonaaaa…

Sam leans her head tenderly on Eric Bishop's shoulder as the celebrations continue. There is a tender private moment between father and daughter as they both sing the same song.

The sound begins to fade but the faces are still animated; Eric looks like a different man among his elated friends.

9. SORTING OFFICE, POST

Early morning shift and the post office is buzzing with the sorting of letters.

Two lines of postmen, perhaps a dozen on each side, are sorting out piles of letters at great speed into some thirty little boxes in front of each man. [They are in a standing position, and piles of letters are dumped on a bench before them. Letters are divided up according to street names which they deliver themselves after sorting.]

Post office workers by the boxes: a blur of nimble dexterity but they can quite easily continue the banter [lots of it] without interfering with speedy coordination between eye and hand.

Eric has the end spot and is obviously battling to keep up. [Perhaps there are worried glances towards him from his immediate workmates COLIN, GINA, and a long-haired mate nicknamed 'THE JUDGE'.]

Spleen, and a big tall guy with bald head called MONK [dead pan and ultra-serious], and JACK [mischievous] study Eric from a strategic spot and can see how he's struggling. He holds letters for seconds too long as if overwhelmed by the choice, and then darts on again, as opposed to the steady rhythm of his mates.

SPLEEN

Look at the state...like a wonky disc...gets
stuck...no rhythm...

JACK

...and getting slower...hard to believe he was a
brilliant dancer...

They notice the office manager watching Eric.

SPLEEN

He's had one warning already.

MONK

Not trying to be funny...but when did
Chrissie leave him?

SPLEEN

About seven years ago...

He shakes his head super solemnly which transfixes the other
two for a moment.

MONK

Won't do...won't do at all...[thinking] That's
over two thousand five hundreds nights on
your own...need a bit of the old ying and
yang...you can't fly in the face of mother
nature...

Jack catches Spleen's eye.

Meatballs marches up to them and pulls a solid book from
inside his jacket. Two others, TRAVIS and SMUG, join the
gang.

MEATBALLS

This is fucking brilliant…will sort Eric out in no time…Come on.

TRAVIS

Oh shit! He's been raiding the 'self-help' section again…you should be banned from bookshops!

Meatballs beckons them to follow them.

IN THE LOCKER ROOM:

Spleen, Monk, Jack, Travis and Smug swarm round Meatballs.

A deeply sceptical Smug grabs the book from Meatballs and reads the title.

SMUG

'INSTANT CONFIDENCE' [underneath] 'The power to go for anything you want'.

He flicks to the back cover and spots a CD.

SMUG (CONT'D)

And…wait for this folks…'Instant Confidence Mind Programming CD'…

TRAVIS

[To Meatballs, exasperated] Jesus…after that last homeopathic cure from one of your books I shat my pants for three months…you're a fucking danger Meatballs!

MEATBALLS

[Grabbing the book back] Give me that! Open up your tiny minds…listen I said!

His powerful presence forces them into silence as he cracks open the book. At last he feels it is appropriate to read the words of wisdom…

                    MEATBALLS (CONT'D)
          'Laughter…even if forced and artificial…has
          been PROVEN to lift our spirits and improve
          our overall mood and well being. It produces
          endorphins to make the body feel good…even
          just smiling [looking up at them] releases
          serotonin into the bloodstream and acts as a
          powerful antidepressant.'

Meatballs stares at his mates who look at him in some confusion.

                         JACK
          Sounds a load of shite…

                      MEATBALLS
          This guy has a PhD!…A scientist of the
          mind…he's proved it with tests…

                       SPLEEN
          On mice or some fucking rabbits…

                        MONK
          In his boots I'd still prefer a good fuck…but
          worth a try…nothing like a laugh when you
          feel like topping yourself…

Jack stares at Monk in amazement.

                      MEATBALLS
          Get to it…cheer him up…and if you can't tell
          him a joke at least fucking smile. Spread the
          word.

They come out of the locker room and observe Eric, still struggling.

In turn, Smug and Spleen, with exaggerated bonhomie, [perhaps with surreal dead pan effort from Monk] come up to Eric and while telling him a short sharp joke, give him a quick hand to sort his letters so he doesn't fall behind.

> THE JUDGE
> Eric…a quick question: What's the difference
> between an egg and wank? [Pause] You can
> beat an egg…but…

From the distance Meatballs nods his approval as several workers round Eric laugh too loudly at the punchline [though all are confused and don't get Monk's contribution].

Perhaps a few pass by Eric and greet him with a warm smile.

Eric barely reacts and simply continues to stare at the sorting boxes as he struggles to put each letter in its appropriate spot.

Another smiler [perhaps Colin] passes and catches his eye.

> ERIC
> Fuck off!

Spleen comes back to Meatballs.

> SPLEEN
> Useless…I remember when Eric told jokes all
> the time…had us in stitches.

> MEATBALLS
> Get a few of the boys together…we'll go up to
> his house after work…cheer him up…

Whether he likes it or not...

10. ERIC'S HOUSE

Meatballs, Spleen, Jack, Travis and Smug walk up the street to Eric's house and knock on the door.

MEATBALLS
Now I'm warning you...no arsing
around...give it a try.

IN THE SITTING ROOM:

Eric [still with scruffy stubble] and his five mates sit back on the soft chairs with their eyes shut.

A CD player in the middle of the table has been turned on.

A plummy voice, in a forlorn attempt at gravitas, tries too hard to sound deep and meaningful – it is accompanied by the cheapest and corniest 'spiritual' music in the background.

VOICE
...Stand in front of your imaginary mirror.
Think of someone who loves you and imagine
viewing yourself through their eyes...

Spleen opens one eye and catches sight of Smug doing the same.

Smug points a finger at Meatballs, squashed up between Travis and Jack. Meatballs, breathing deeply, has his head arched back, mouth slightly open, gut hanging out, while the more compact Travis has his head bowed down as if meditating and maybe his legs crossed in a forlorn attempt at the Lotus position. Jack, beside them, has his worried face determinedly set at 'serious'.

Travis opens an eye now too and tentatively checks to make sure Meatballs isn't watching him.

> VOICE (CONT'D)
> ...gently press the thumb of each hand gently
> against the longest finger...

They all fuck it up totally with various combinations [thumb of right hand against longest finger on the left etc, Jack with thumb on index finger etc] till they all copy Eric [which encourages Meatballs] who gets it right.

> VOICE (CONT'D)
> Now...with eyes closed...breathing
> slowly...deep breaths...[especially from
> Meatballs] allow yourself to really see yourself
> through the eyes of someone who totally loves
> you...

Smug, Spleen, and Travis start to crack as they catch sight of Meatballs breathing even more heavily.

> VOICE (CONT'D)
> ...who totally accepts you as you are...who
> loves you without condition...

Spleen bites his fingers furiously as his red face is about to explode while Travis, in the danger zone beside Meatballs, crunches up and smothers his mouth with his hand.

Meatballs, in deep frustration, clicks off the tape and stares at them in thunderous mood daring them to challenge him. They quieten down and manage to control themselves. He snaps up the book and opens it at a marker.

MEATBALLS

[Reading] 'The Possibility Generator'...[with a
dark flash of his eyes, warning] Think of
someone whose confidence and charisma you
wish to emulate...

Meatballs nods at them to do it.

MEATBALLS (CONT'D)

Right...have you all got someone?...Who is it?

SMUG

Still thinking...

MEATBALLS

Jesus...you got the whole fucking world to
choose from...You?

JACK

It's private...

MEATBALLS

Who the fuck is it?

JACK

Nelson Mandela...

TRAVIS

The Dalai Lama...

SPLEEN

Karl Marx...

MEATBALLS

Bollocks! Can you not think of someone alive
and under ninety!

SMUG

Can it be a combination of characters?

MEATBALLS

Jesus Christ! Just choose one! Right you too
Eric…[Eric just stares ahead and doesn't
answer] think of someone…Now…[back to
book] 'Go over to your role model…[slowly,
meaningfully] and float into their body…'

SPLEEN

Can I change mine to Marilyn Monroe?

MEATBALLS

Fuck! Shut it! [Order restored] '…float into
their body and synchronise with their
posture…'

Smug has a filthy grin on his face, flicks his tongue along his
mouth and slightly gyrates his pelvis at Spleen who tries his
best not to roar again.

Jack notices a partly open door to Eric's cupboard. His face
changes. He jumps up and pulls the door fully open. Hundreds
of unopened letters tumble out.

JACK

Fuck…

They all turn to stare at Eric.

JACK

Eric…how long has this been going on?

Eric drops his gaze. Nothing.

See if you can find some plastic bags…call the
boys and we'll get these out tomorrow. [To
Eric] I give up…[he throws the book down in
resignation] You've got to speak to someone
Eric…

11. ERIC'S HOUSE – NIGHT

Eric, in his flannel striped pyjamas, sneaks down the stairs in
the middle of the night.

He approaches Ryan's room and peeks inside.

The TV is on and the light from it illuminates Ryan's sleeping
face. His girlfriend is tucked up beside him and she is fast
asleep too.

Eric bends down and gingerly rolls up a Man United rug laid
out in front of the bed.

Nervously, he unpicks a loose floorboard which creaks loudly
on extraction.

From inside the secret hiding place he steals a little dope and
closes it all up again.

He sneaks out again up to his own room.

Eric, still dressed in his pyjamas, and sitting on a seat opposite
the cardboard cut-out of Cantona, takes some mighty puffs
from a fat joint.

He can feel the effect run through him in an instant.

Meatballs' voice from earlier in the evening rings in his ears as
Eric stands up and moves closer to the cut-out of Cantona.

MEATBALLS VOICE OVER

...float into their body...[copying and imitating Cantona] by standing...breathing... smiling...talking and moving the way your role model does...[he moves round the room with his chest stuck out] you'll begin to develop the same quality of thoughts and internal states as they do. You will begin to transform your experience of being alive...

Eric moves back to confront the poster: re-arranging his feet he copies the body first, then chest, and then he concentrates on the face. He tries to capture the scowl and confident look in his eyes.

At last he moves closer, and then flicks up the collar of his pyjamas.

ERIC

Flawed genius eh?...[Pause] Flawed postman...

Eric stares at Cantona, eye to eye.

ERIC (CONT'D)

How's your 'self care' Eric? Have you ever thought of killing yourself?...Can you imagine your life in five years? [Pause] Who loves you Eric...takes care of you? [Silence for a moment. He moves away, long pause] But do you know the one that knocked me for six?...Didn't see it fucking coming...'Have you ever done anything you are ashamed of?'

Eric stares into space, thinking, remembering. A long moment.

CANTONA'S VOICE

Well…have you?

Eric turns round quickly in a confused fashion. He moves closer and closer to the poster.

ERIC

Was that you?

CANTONA'S VOICE

[Behind him] Yes…it was me.

Eric swivels round.

ERIC CANTONA, now forty, sits back nice and relaxed on one of the soft seats beside the sofa.

Eric stares at him. Stunned. He takes a step closer. Then another. He gently stretches out a hand and touches Cantona's arm and then, with a finger, gently taps his skull.

ERIC

Fuck fuck fuck…

Eric stares at the cardboard cut-out and then back at the real man.

ERIC (CONT'D)

Is that…really really you?

CANTONA

Yip.

ERIC

[Testing, distrustful] Say something in French.

CANTONA

Je suis…Eric Cantona.

ERIC

Wait till the lads hear about this...they still
fucking love you!

CANTONA

Thank you.

ERIC

Who would believe...

CANTONA

[Cutting him off] It's Lily...n'est-ce pas?

Eric is dumbstruck. He struggles and shakes his head.

CANTONA (CONT'D)

Can't even say her name. [Pause] Say it.

But Cantona, with those same eyes that struck fear into the
opposition, won't let him off.

ERIC

Lily...yeah...always Lily...

CANTONA

You have to face this...

ERIC

I can't...[tapping his own chest] Nobody in.
Where did I go? [Pause] Funny that...Eric
Bishop...washed away...

CANTONA

Ah...feeling a little bit sorry for yourself?

ERIC

Feel nothing...[pointing to cut-out] Like you
up there...that's me...

Cantona stares across at an old wooden trunk in the corner of his room. Eric shakes his head.

                    CANTONA
        Well?

                    ERIC
        I can't...

                    CANTONA
        Open the trunk Eric...

Eric, deeply disturbed at the thought, continues to shake his head.

                    CANTONA (CONT'D)
        [In French] 'Without danger...we cannot get
        beyond danger'.

Eric is confused until Cantona, hesitatingly, translates.

                    CANTONA (CONT'D)
        Old proverb. [Pause] Open it.

Eric stubbornly stares.

Cantona marches over, swipes the rubbish from on top and hurls open the lid.

                    CANTONA (CONT'D)
        Maybe you're in here Eric?

Again he holds his eye. Long pause.

                    CANTONA (CONT'D)
        Come on...

At last Eric comes over. He looks in tentatively.

He reaches in and pulls out miscellaneous files and envelopes.

ERIC

My God...

Stuffed down the side of the trunk he extracts something in a glass frame covered in dust. He wipes his sleeve over it to reveal a photograph and article from a local newspaper with headline 'Manchester couple win competition at 50s night'.

Eric stares down at the black and white images of a handsome young man and gorgeous girl dressed like fifties Rockers. They are beaming in delight. She holds up a trophy and he holds up a magnum bottle of champagne.

CANTONA

[Reading] '19th of July 1979'...[counting for what seems like an age in French with fingers and thumbs, at last]...thirty years ago...

Eric is transfixed by it, almost trembling.

ERIC

Thirty...Jesus...was that me? [Pause] I loved dancing...rock and roll...getting the gear on...the hair done...one of those mock fifties competitions...My God...what a night...

CANTONA

What a pair of blue suede shoes.

ERIC

Got them sent from America...cost me a week's wages...wonder what ever happened to them...

CANTONA

[Reading again] 'Eric Bishop and Lily Devine triumph…' Mon Dieu! A blind date! Très romantique…

ERIC

Yeah…knocked me for six.

Eric bites his lip as he stares again at their former selves.

CANTONA

Sometimes the beautiful memories are the [struggling for the word]…plus plus…most toughest of them all…

Eric's eyes flick up in grateful recognition.

ERIC

Yeah…

A long moment between them.

ERIC (CONT'D)

…Daft idea…talked into it by my mates…the compère pulled numbers at random from a box…and we met on the dance floor for the first time…'Number 19…Eric…where are you?' I came out to the dance floor…nervous as hell…'And for the girls…number 1…Lily!' he shouted…I remember her number…there was a long pause and I thought…fuck…she's sizing me up…I could be left standing here like a prick…and then I turned…Man…she just floated out…absolutely gorgeous…shy… but you could sense mischief too…we went mad…I tossed her about and she came flying back faster every time…she trusted me…the crowd went crazy…the music stopped…her chest was heaving…and I held her…

Long pause as Eric looks at the picture again.

12. FLASHBACK – ROCK N ROLL COMPETITION

[Black and white, impressionistic – snippets of the night.]

A fifties night competition. Men are dressed like Elvis and the girls are in flouncy dresses.

Each competitor has a number round their shoulders.

The compère pulls a number at random from a box and the boys and girls meet each other on the dance floor for the first time.

COMPERE

Number 19! Eric…where are you?

Eric, athletic, compact, confident, strides onto the dance floor to join another dozen couples. He waits expectantly for his partner.

COMPERE (CONT'D)

And for the girls…number 1! Lily!

Eric turns to watch Lily Devine emerge from the mass for the first time.

Eye to eye. Immediate attraction, but still a shyness as they move closer.

DANCE: Rock and roll number.

They move freely, at ease from the first.

Number ends. A moment between them.

ANOTHER NUMBER – but much faster.

Eric twirls, hurls and pulls Lily back and forward at great speed. She matches him. Trusts him. Faster and faster.

The crowd notice their talent and clap at some of the more extravagant moves. Their confidence together grows.

She jumps and Eric, like a juggler, flicks her round his back to catch her again…

ANOTHER NUMBER – perhaps now in slow motion and much closer. The music stops and loud cheers.

Eric and Lily, their chests heaving and faces running with sweat, stare at each other.

> ERIC
> …it was that look in her eye…the smell of perfume…her sweat…her dress was soaked through. I could feel the dancer's muscles along her back…down her side…her tight waist…my hand slipped to her hip and she just…smiled…that first smile…Fuck! That was it. I knew we'd be together. At the end of the night I didn't even ask her…she heard me on the phone ordering my best mate to get out of his flat and leave the key under the mat…and she laughed…and he did…

ERIC'S ROOM:

Cantona listens as Eric continues.

> ERIC (CONT'D)
> We met a few more times but it didn't take long…

13. FLASHBACK – A BEDROOM

Two beautiful youngsters, bodies at their prime, anticipate a night together.

Eric sits on a chair at one side of a bed while Lily sits on another at the far side.

Lily shyly looks up at him. They stare at each other for an age. More smiles and trembling, unbearable excitement between them. [Perhaps tentative singing between them from the number – below – they have just danced to, accompanied by mini-striptease of shoes, pendants, buttons, etc until a point they both feel comfortable.]

                    ERIC (CONT'D)
[Quietly, singing] Look up...

                    LILY
[Answering] Look up...

                    ERIC
Is that the moon we see...can't be...

                    LILY
Can't be...

                    ERIC
Looks like the sun to me...it's late...

                    LILY
It's late...

                    ERIC
I'd hate to face your dad...too bad...

                    LILY
...too bad...

ERIC

I know he's going to be mad…it's late…

LILY

It's late…We gotta get on home…

ERIC

It's late…

LILY

It's late…

ERIC AND LILY

We've been gone too long…

Lily delicately pulls her foot up onto the bed and takes off her shoe – on sudden impulse she hurls it at him which makes him laugh.

He undoes a blue suede shoe. He tosses it at her and she catches it.

They repeat with their other shoes.

More mischief between them. Lily stretches out her leg on the bed and wiggles her toes. Grins between them.

Eric undoes the first button of his shirt.

Lily takes off the pendant from around her neck.

More long looks between them as they just hold each other's shining eyes.

CANTONA VOICE OVER

And that was it…

ERIC VOICE OVER

Maybe it was the dancing…we rolled into
one…just one of those magical nights you can
never have again…Sometimes we didn't say a
word for a long long time…just watched…
held each other's eye…I've never done that
with anyone else but Lily Devine.

BACK TO ERIC'S ROOM – PRESENT:

A long moment between Eric and Cantona.

CANTONA

'Si jeunesse savait, si vieillesse pouvait.' [Pause]
How do you say…'Youth is wasted on the
young.'

Eric ponders and remembers.

ERIC

Wasn't wasted…will stay with me forever.

CANTONA

What did she like most about you?

Eric, sombre, waits for a moment.

ERIC

I made her laugh.

CANTONA

And thirty years later…you can't even face her.

14. FLASHBACK – A WEEK AGO – SAM'S HOME

Eric's daughter SAM [aged twenty-seven] sits in a little back
garden of a council house.

Eric sits beside her having a cup of tea. He rocks his grandchild DAISY [seven months] on his knee as he feeds her from a bottle.

> SAM
>
> Dad...I want to ask you a big big favour...

Eric looks up.

> SAM (CONT'D)
>
> Just two months till my final exams...I'm struggling...way behind...and going to fail...know what this means to me?

Eric nods.

> SAM (CONT'D)
>
> I'm just wondering...after you pick Daisy from the nursery...instead of bringing her back here at five like you normally do...can you keep her for just one more hour till six?

> ERIC
>
> No problem...she's a little beauty...

> SAM
>
> I'm going to be in the library every night till ten...study like hell...just six weeks...that's all...

> ERIC
>
> So where will I drop her?

Long pause.

> SAM
>
> At Mum's.

Eric jumps up involuntarily and walks around with the baby.

> ### ERIC
>
> For God's sake Sam! I can't do that…I've
> hardly seen your mum in years…most of your
> lifetime for Christ's sake! You can't ask me
> that…not now…it's too…

He can't finish.

> ### SAM
>
> Dad…you've both moved on…It doesn't make
> sense! I see you both all the time…I spoke to
> Mum and she doesn't mind…

Long moment.

> ### ERIC
>
> What did she say?

> ### SAM
>
> Practical…by far the easiest.

> ### ERIC
>
> What did she say?

> ### SAM
>
> She said it might be good to see you again…
> catch up.

Eric stares at her for a long moment.

Sam is embarrassed by her lie. A long silence.

> ### ERIC
>
> Was she upset?

Sam shakes her head.

ERIC (CONT'D)

Tell me exactly what she said...

SAM

'It doesn't really matter anymore...'

It knocks him for six. His head drops.

SAM (CONT'D)

Well you asked! Dad...she just wants to help me...

Silence for a long moment.

ERIC

What about your neighbour?

SAM

It's four hours...far too much!

ERIC

Can I not drop her off at Steve's? Just till the exams are over...

Sam withdraws into herself.

SAM

I won't see that bastard ever again...

Sam can see that Eric is struggling.

SAM (CONT'D)

He's not like you were Dad...never sends a penny...doesn't give a shit.

ERIC

Really hard for me...things you don't understand sweetheart...

SAM

Come on Dad…meet her…get it over and
done with. I've got to pass the exams this
time…I won't ever have to depend on
Steve…will change my life.

Sam looks at him. He can hardly bear the desperation in her
face.

SAM (CONT'D)

There's no one else I can rely on…

ERIC

Sam…not at my best…look at me…I can't
face your mum just now…

SAM

Just a handover…as simple as that…I need you
both.

The phone rings from inside and Sam lays the baby on Eric's
lap. Eric hugs her and kisses the top of her head.

ERIC

'It doesn't really matter anymore…' [To Daisy]
Eh?

BACK TO ERIC'S ROOM:

Eric and Cantona sit opposite each other.

ERIC (CONT'D)

So many mistakes…so much water under the
bridge…Jesus…can you imagine being asked
by your daughter to meet your ex-wife on a
daily basis whom you've hardly seen in three
decades?

71

CANTONA

Un petit…how do you say…'shock'.

ERIC

Un 'petit' shock…More like the man on death row strapped to an electric fucking chair in Texas!…But you know what sunk me?…I asked her if Lily was upset at the idea of meeting me…I wondered if she was nervous. Sam lied at first…and then I asked her to tell me exactly what Lily said…five words…

Eric shakes his head.

ERIC (CONT'D)

'It doesn't really matter anymore'…that's what she said. [Pause] It's worse than hatred!

CANTONA

Oui. Much worse…

ERIC

Thank you…

CANTONA

What do you expect after all this time? A Hollywood script?

Long pause. He looks shamed.

ERIC

…and then when I saw her [pause] she'd really taken care of herself…her hair…the way she stood…everything…but you know what really got me?

FLASHBACK (AS SCENE 3):

Eric peeks at Lily from behind the pillar, torn between tenderness and terror.

ERIC (CONT'D)
...the way she dressed...it was so simple and I know she didn't want to embarrass me...she knows I've been through hell...she didn't want to rub my nose in it...

CANTONA
So she does care...

It stops Eric for a moment.

ERIC
...I could sense her kindness [pause]...the baby must have woken up...she leaned in and just laughed...so tender...fuck...

Eric darts back behind the pillar and leans against it as he tries to calm himself.

He can't force himself to face her and walks off.

BACK TO ERIC'S ROOM:

Cantona stares at Eric.

CANTONA
Brought it all back...you...Lily and baby Sam?

Eric nods, stunned.

ERIC
Like yesterday...almost thirty years.

Long pause.

CANTONA

What about Sam now? [Eric cringes] Her
exams? Are you going to help her?

Eric sinks into himself. Long silence.

Cantona leans over and takes the spliff from Eric. He takes an
enormous draw – lasting several seconds which nearly finishes
the entire spliff – and then hands him back the stump. Eric
examines the remnants.

ERIC

I'm fucked...

CANTONA

Oui...[Pause] I suggest a very high building
...or head in the oven like a...how do you
say...big goose...Ah...[eyes lighting up] how
about Madame Guillotine?

ERIC

All right for you!...'Flawed' genius bastard
playing beach football...V.I.P...celebrity
pals...even got a French accent! Look at
me...scrawny as fuck...You've got it all!

Pause.

CANTONA

Do you think my friends are better than
yours?

Long silence, and then it all bursts out in a torrent.

ERIC

It's all slipping through my fingers...the boys
look through me...I can't trust myself...feel

I'm floating…look down on myself…
wandering around like a scabby old dog…I
feel scared all the time and don't know why…

CANTONA

We all feel scared sometimes…

ERIC

I'm losing it!

CANTONA

[In French first, pause, and then translated] 'He
that forecasts all perils…will never sail the seas.'

Eric struggles with it.

CANTONA (CONT'D)

'He that is afraid to shake the dice…will never
throw a six…' [Warming to another after the
spliff] 'If you do not enter a tiger's den…[but
cut off before he reaches the conclusion] you
cannot get his cubs…'

ERIC

Stick your proverbs up your arse! How do you
say that in French?

A moment between them.

CANTONA

Always got more choices than we think.
Always.

Eric shakes his head.

ERIC

Like what?!

CANTONA

A shave.

Eric shakes his head.

ERIC

I can't face her.

Cantona's dark eyes pin him.

15. SHOPPING PRECINCT

Eric, looking very different with a smart haircut, fresh shave, and clean shirt, marches with determination.

He peers at Lily and pram from behind a shop doorway as he builds up his courage.

ERIC

[Whispered to himself] Come on you useless prick...

He walks towards her. She looks up at him.

ERIC (CONT'D)

Hi Chrissie...

LILY

First wife...Lily.

ERIC

Ahh fuck...

Rather than her hurt he feels her profound distance.

ERIC (CONT'D)

I'm sorry...just a bit nervous...

LILY

It doesn't matter Eric…

It really strikes him.

LILY (CONT'D)

[Looking down at the baby] She fed about half an hour ago…[pointing under the pram] I've got fruit purée in the tupperware and the nappies are under here too. I think she'll sleep…she's had a busy morning…haven't you darling?

ERIC

Great…excellent…

LILY

The bib's under there too and a bottle of water if she needs it…

ERIC

Fantastic!

Lily looks at him. A moment between them.

LILY

Are you okay Eric?

ERIC

Fine…fine…sorry about the other day…a dizzy spell and conked out…overtime…the boys…hadn't slept…but back to normal. Fighting fit.

Her eyes survey him quickly. She nods. She doesn't challenge him but he knows she can see through him.

LILY

Are you okay for bringing her to my place
later or would you prefer to meet here?

Eric tries his best to be casual.

ERIC

Whatever's easiest…it's only six weeks…

Again he realises he's put his foot in it.

LILY

Yeah…

ERIC

I didn't mean that…

They take refuge by looking down at Daisy. Long awkward silence.

ERIC (CONT'D)

Have you got time for a cup of tea Lily?

LILY

Why?

She looks at him but he can hardly bear it. Eric squirms as he struggles for the words. She puts him out of his misery.

LILY (CONT'D)

Let's just try and get through this as best we
can for Sam…I'll see you later Eric. [To Daisy]
Bye sweetheart…

She walks off as Eric takes over baby duties. He watches her disappear into the distance.

Eric picks up Daisy and holds her close. He gives her a tender kiss. He has one last glance at Lily.

16. ERIC'S HOUSE

Eric, in his uniform, overladen with plastic shopping bags bulging with groceries, approaches the front garden to his home. He can see three youths push something very heavy on wheels, covered by thick tarpaulin.

By the time he gets to the garden, the boys are inside the house.

He disentangles himself from the plastic bags, and moves over to the piece of machinery. He whips off the tarpaulin to reveal a huge cement mixer.

He stares at it for several moments.

He moves inside. The TV booms from the sitting room. Again, it is a total mess. Ryan and his three mates sit and watch a video. They are all dressed in Man U colours.

> ERIC
> Ryan...I want a word...

He ignores Eric.

> ERIC (CONT'D)
> [Shouting] What the fuck is that out there?

> RYAN
> Just a rough guess...but it looks like a cement
> mixer.

His three mates roll about laughing.

Suddenly there is the wild pumping of a car horn outside.

The boys run out and start singing a Man U song. Eric follows Ryan into the hall as the latter pulls a Man U scarf over his shoulder from a rack.

ERIC

Get that bloody mixer out of here before you
go...What if the police see it?

RYAN

Chill out man...it'll be gone in an hour.
[From the step] Next time I'll try and get
you a ticket Eric...a promise...Zac goes to one
of the best boxes in the stadium...champagne
...the works man...you'll love it...

A sharply dressed muscular man, ZAC, [thirty at the most] in
the driver's seat beckons them as the music booms from the
speakers. He is accompanied by his sidekick BUSBY.
[Compact, physical, and the same age.]

ZAC

Arse into gear!

BUSBY

[To Ryan] Come on skinny...move it!

Eric watches them scramble into a luxury black Mercedes
Benz which accelerates off at great speed.

Eric notices more miscellaneous gear leaning up against the
wall in the hall. He picks up what looks like some sort of fake
gun for adventure weekends. His curiosity gets the better of
him. He aims at his postman's jacket hanging on the rack. He
can't help but pull the trigger. There is an earsplitting blast as
he covers it – and half the wall – in a huge splurge of red paint.

ERIC

[Examining jacket] Fuck! Fuck! Fuck it!

5

6

7

8

9

10

11

12

13

14

15

16

17

18

19

20

21

22

23

24

17. ERIC'S ROOM – NIGHT

Cantona, slightly bemused and concerned, stares at Eric as he throws miscellaneous private bits and pieces [quirky possessions including a dark brown overall with letters 'JB' embroidered on the pocket, as well as papers, letters, photographs etc] from his trunk. Cantona spots a photograph of a man wearing the same overalls, outside a shop, standing proudly beside his greyhound.

> CANTONA
> Your father? [Eric nods] Were you close?

> ERIC
> He once sat on me by mistake.

Eric takes the photograph and examines the man.

> ERIC (CONT'D)
> All his affection went to that dog…

> CANTONA
> Playing safe…

Eric is confused.

> CANTONA (CONT'D)
> A dog doesn't reject you. Maybe he was scared too?

It stops Eric in his tracks for a moment.

Cantona picks up the overalls.

> CANTONA (CONT'D)
> Why did you keep this?

Eric examines it momentarily. He looks at the initials, JB.

ERIC

Jack Bishop…[confused, hurt] I don't know.

He shakes his head as he examines another photograph of his father.

CANTONA

Sometimes we miss what we never had…

ERIC

My tenth birthday…I remember him telling
jokes with his mates. They were laughing their
heads off…apparently he was very witty. I
smiled too…made a half step to join them…a
flick of those dark eyes…as if 'Don't you dare'
and he turned his back…stopped me in my
tracks. [Pause] Then 'Dandy Boy' when I
started the dancing…always that look of semi
disgust…but my Mum loved it…made her
laugh. Sometimes we'd dance in the kitchen
when the old sod went to bed.

Eric continues to dig inside the trunk.

Finally Eric discovers an envelope with just the word Lily written on it at the very bottom of the trunk.

Eric stares at it for a long moment and then hands it to Cantona. Cantona examines the word Lily but doesn't open it.

ERIC (CONT'D)

She sent me this the week after I left her…

Cantona looks at him – Eric nods – and then opens the envelope. Inside there is a postcard. [Very distinctive, a simple sketch by Picasso of a dove, with a yellow sun above it. The dove carries an olive twig in its mouth.] Cantona turns it over.

CANTONA

[Reading] 'I can't love you any more than this.
[Pause] Lily'.

A moment between them.

ERIC

I never ever answered her. The longer I left it
the worse it was. There's no way back from that.

Cantona just looks at him.

CANTONA

And you haven't stopped thinking about her…

Eric sinks into himself again.

CANTONA (CONT'D)

Tell her the truth…

ERIC

Problem with the truth…sometimes it's
unfuckingbelievable!! What can you say to
someone who laid their heart out on a plate…
There's just no words…no way round it. It's
just there…for ever.

Eric snaps the postcard from Cantona.

ERIC (CONT'D)

Fuck it!

He tears it in two, tosses it into the fireplace.

ERIC (CONT'D)

I'm never going to get through this! How can
I meet her every day? I'll be back to that
fucking roundabout…

CANTONA

Speak to her...

ERIC

I can't!

CANTONA

Write to her...

Eric shakes his head in exasperation.

ERIC

I've got no words...

Silence. Outside, through the open window, they can hear voices.

MEATBALLS

Eric. Are you up there? Eric!

Silence.

CANTONA

I think they mean you...

Eric ignores them.

JACK

Can see your light on. We're going for a
pint...come on! The game's on Sky.

MONK

If you don't come down...we'll come up and
grab you!

CANTONA

You are a lucky man...

Cantona throws Eric his jacket.

84

As Eric puts on his jacket he is now alone in the empty room.

18. PUB – EVENING

Ordinary local pub, and the majority of the clientele are Man U fans [wearing their tops] waiting for their game to be shown on Sky.

Eric [down, but gradually drawn out of himself a little bit by the vitality of his mates] is there with Meatballs, Monk, Jack, Smug, Travis, Colin and The Judge who is wearing a Man U jersey. [Spleen, wearing a FC United football top, will let off steam and be true to his nickname while some of the others wind him up. Some have sympathy for his position, but don't have the willpower to follow through as he suggests. Meatballs and Monk notice Eric smile for the first time and take heart at his progress.]

A couple of Man U fans, MICKEY and DENIS, spot Spleen, with his FC United shirt, carrying a tray of pints back to his mates above.

MICKEY
Look at that shirt! Wouldn't wipe my arse with that.

DENIS
'Football Club United!'…'Fucking Clowns United!' if you ask me…bunch of traitors…ran off and left us…

SPLEEN
[Fury] You're the fucking traitors! Selling off our club to the fat cats! Are you blind? It's not yours anymore!

COLIN

Calm down Spleen for God's sake! Give
yourself a heart-attack…

SPLEEN

I never left United…

DENIS

Yes you did…you ran off!

SPLEEN

They left me…

They laugh and take the piss.

THE JUDGE

…The most popular club in history…330
million fans around the world! And they left
you!

COLIN

Very inconsiderate…

THE JUDGE

Listen…listen…'In this life a man can change
his wife…political party or his religion…but
he can never change his favourite football
team'. Galeano…a real philosopher…

SPLEEN

Yeah…and he's the twat that thought the earth
went round the sun…

JACK

It fucking does!!

TRAVIS

Come on Spleen...admit it...three years ago
you ran off with a bunch of troublemakers
formed a mini-me-social club who couldn't fill
a public toilet...you're too small...no roots...
never last...

MEATBALLS

That's what they said about United...How did
it start? 1878!...Newton Heath it was
called...humble railway workers...you've
pissed on your own history!

SPLEEN

How can you sell your club to the Yanks way
over the fucking Pacific ocean...

MONK

Atlantic...

SPLEEN

...money money money...that's all they care
about...

THE JUDGE

Rubbish! [Tapping his heart, and Man U top]
It's in here!

SPLEEN

[Fury] Car parks don't lie!

Eric can't but help smile at Monk's confused expression.

MONK

True...when you think about it...

SPLEEN

Have you seen the type of car in there on
match days? [Now Monk gets it]...No
postmen now...I'll tell you that...name anyone
from our time who can afford a season ticket?

JACK

Up the Revolution!

SPLEEN

Yeah...[kissing his shirt] Our club! We set it
up...modest I know...but we own it! We
decide! No fat bastard chairman can sell us out
for thirty pieces of silver!

Some of the fans laugh at his outburst.

JACK

Three years old...no history!

SPLEEN

We took the soul of Man United with us to FC
and left you with the fucking prawn cocktails!
We took the memories...the spirit...even the
songs...

SMUG

Pity you never took some of the players...

MONK

And the stadium.

SPLEEN

...no fucking history...eh?

SPLEEN AND MEATBALLS

[Singing]…'Won't pay for Glazer, or work for
Sky, still sing "City's gonna die", two Uniteds
but the soul is one, as the Busby Babes carry
on. Glazer wherever you may be, you bought
Old Trafford but you can't buy me, I sang
"Not for Sale" and I meant just that, you can't
buy me you greedy twat!'

This draws more laughter and slagging in equal measure.

DENIS

Bunch of nutters…How many do you get at a
home game?

SPLEEN

At least three thousand…maybe more…

Several of the fans burst out laughing and some whistle in
mock admiration.

THE JUDGE

Got the toilets built yet?

SPLEEN

At least I can go to a game and take my two
sons…can you do that? And half our fans are
under eighteen! [Not letting The Judge off]
When was the last time you were at a game?
Come on…tell me!

THE JUDGE

Rather see it on the telly…and enjoy a pint if
you'd give me peace…

SPLEEN

Not the same! [To Eric] Me and Meatballs go
every Saturday…

MEATBALLS

Fantastic Eric…like the old days on the bus…
singing…really close…give it a try…bring the
boys…only two quid.

A shout comes up in the pub as the Man U team runs on to the
pitch on screen.

Spleen's eyes like everyone else are stuck to the set as Ronaldo
and Rooney warm up. [Perhaps a close-up of a sponsor or
expensive advert.]

MEATBALLS

Daylight robbery…[looking up at the telly,
genuine sadness, shared by Spleen]…They
went right into our Saturday afternoon and
ripped our hearts out…then into our living
rooms and stole our game…

SPLEEN

…and here you are on a Monday night
disgracing yourselves to keep that fucker
Murdoch happy…

MONK

So you won't be watching then?

SPLEEN

Wouldn't give the bastards the drips off my
nose…Edwards walks off with sixty million!
Up at Newcastle the Halls grab a hundred
million…Spurs…Alan Sugar fifty million…

COLIN

[Cutting him off] Sit back and relax!

SPLEEN

Relax!!!

THE JUDGE

Shut the fuck up and let us watch the game!

SPLEEN

Bunch of useless vegetables…no wonder they
get away with it…Come on Meatballs…let's
get out of here!

Meatballs' face falls and some of them laugh.

MEATBALLS

Just got to finish my pint Spleen…

They all turn to stare at Spleen whose eyes reluctantly follow
the screen. The whistle blows for the kick off.

DENIS

You'll be off then?

SPLEEN

Damn right!

SMUG

No collaboration with the fat cats…

SPLEEN

Telling me…

TRAVIS

A man of principle…

Spleen is beginning to weaken.

91

COLIN

Off to walk the dog then…

They are all grinning like mad as Spleen reluctantly slinks out. The boys catch each other's eye. Just as Spleen leaves the pub with a last lingering look at the telly, and the door swings closed, they all jump up and shout 'Goal!!'

Spleen dives in again so quickly he sends someone inside flying with the force of the door.

SPLEEN

Who scored?! Who scored?!

They all piss themselves in laughter as they see him stare up at the screen with all the enthusiasm of old.

He catches sight of their mirth.

SPLEEN (CONT'D)

Bastards!

He wanders back, forlorn, and slumps down on the same chair.

SPLEEN (CONT'D)

Fuck it…I miss them so much…

Eric chuckles as he pours out half his pint into Spleen's empty glass.

Eric stares round at the faces of his mates with eyes stuck to the telly, and appreciates them for a moment.

19. STREET AND ERIC'S HOME – NIGHT

Eric walks home by himself from the pub.

As he gets closer to his house he can see a distinctive black Mercedes Benz pulled up outside the front door. Busby sits on the bonnet, waiting. Eric stops and watches from behind a car. [He is too far to hear what is said but the body language is clear.]

Eric can see Zac and Ryan outside the front door. Zac talks at speed and gives Ryan a good bollocking, although he doesn't shout. Ryan answers him nervously, and to Eric's shock, Zac gives Ryan a vicious slap across the face. More gesticulating. He then grabs him roughly by the ear. Total humiliation.

Zac leaves Ryan and climbs into the car with Busby. They shoot off.

Ryan, forlorn, heads back inside the house.

Eric moves closer and enters. The cement mixer has gone.

Ryan is getting something from the fridge. Eric joins him and sits down at the kitchen table.

Ryan says nothing, but he looks really shaken. Silence between them for some time.

ERIC
Remember we used to talk about everything?

RYAN
Too late for that...

ERIC
What's he want from you?

The question hangs in the air.

RYAN

He's been good to me…

ERIC

So good he smacks you in the face…Is that a
friend these days?

Ryan withdraws into himself.

ERIC (CONT'D)

I want to help you Ryan…we can't go on like
this…

RYAN

What can you do Eric?

Ryan walks out and the front door slams.

Hearing the sound of laughter, Eric goes upstairs and peers
into Jess's room. Jess and two teenagers have their eyes stuck to
a computer screen. They are highly excited and riveted by the
material.

ERIC

Right boys…it's late…got to go home…

They don't even hear him.

Between their heads Eric can see on screen several masked
teenagers messing around and playing with two hand guns.

Jess and the boys, oblivious to Eric, have a running
commentary between them as to the possible identity of the
gang and endless technical detail about the type of gun and its
attributes.

ERIC (CONT'D)

Five minutes boys…and that's it…

IN THE KITCHEN:

Eric silently washes another huge pile of filthy dishes.

As he leans over to grab a burnt pot he catches sight of Cantona sitting at the kitchen table staring at him. His dark eyes brood.

Cantona shakes his head slowly.

CANTONA

[Quietly] 'No'.

Eric looks at him. Cantona encourages him to say it.

CANTONA (CONT'D)

'No'.

More encouragement. Again, 'No'. Eric struggles to get the word out but he can't do it.

CANTONA (CONT'D)

Come on...say it...'No'!

He tries harder but it is beyond him. Cantona encourages him but Eric's lips are sealed.

CANTONA (CONT'D)

In French...'Non'.

After a struggle Eric manages a timid 'Non' [accent perfectly copied].

Cantona jumps up. Demonstrating. With energy.

CANTONA (CONT'D)

From your balls. 'Non'!!

Eric gets it out a little louder.

Cantona encourages with his hand. Eric manages to say it again. More encouragement by Cantona.

The word builds and builds. Eric, staring at the soap suds, begins to force himself to say it.

ERIC
[Louder and faster] Non! Non! Non! Non!

He grabs a ladle and starts pounding it like fuck off the bench in time with the word which he howls now from the top of his lungs.

ERIC (CONT'D)
Non! Non! Non! Non! Non! Non!

Eric looks up.

Now total silence.

Jess and his two mates, caught between curiosity and fear, stare at the lone figure of Eric from the kitchen door.

MATE 1
Let's get the fuck out of here…

The two mates run off. Long moment.

JESS
Eric…are you okay?

ERIC
[Quietly again] Non.

20. STREETS AND BLOCKS OF FLATS

[Split reality scene. Eric carries out his deliveries in various locations, from shops, terraces to high-rises.

As he plods along in his routine Cantona accompanies him, as a friend might do.

Cantona, of course, is only present for Eric – no one else.

When Eric is with other people in the street or at a door, Cantona is not there. But if Eric is in the stairwell of a high-rise, there should be casual chat between them.]

They are mid-conversation about some of his best goals. Eric remembers them all, while Cantona struggles.

ERIC
Remember that one against Aston Villa?

CANTONA
No...

ERIC
Right...West Ham? Your third season?

CANTONA
No...

And so it continues between the deliveries.

As they climb a high zigzagged stairwell Cantona gives him a hand with the letters sticking them through the post boxes.

ERIC
...must have been amazing...fifty thousand all watching you...cheering...chanting your name!

CANTONA

Scary...

ERIC

You! Scared!...Never!

Cantona turns to him.

CANTONA

Scared it might stop...

Eric looks at him. He stops in his tracks.

CANTONA (CONT'D)

I loved to surprise the crowd...I tried to offer
them a gift...Sometimes it wouldn't happen...
but sometimes it did. I could feel the energy!
Fifty thousand souls connect...a magic
moment...Woom!

ERIC

In our minds for ever...

CANTONA

But I had to surprise myself first...take a
risk...depends on the limits you set yourself...
play safe...and no gift...

They both sit on a step.

ERIC

Remember Sunderland?

Cantona smiles.

Sound of football chants from thousands.

FADES INTO FLASHBACK:

That wondrous goal and moment of sheer elation. [Cantona dribbles round two players in midfield – crowd roars in expectation – lays it off to McClair who slots it back. Cantona looks up and chips a swerving beauty over the goalkeeper which hits a sweet spot just inside the top corner.] The crowd roars as Cantona struts.

FADE BACK TO THE STEPS:

                    ERIC (CONT'D)
          [Savouring] Beauty…'Magnifique' [Cantona
          glances at him impressed]…Like a dance…
          Kept me going for months that goal…it fills
          you up so much you forget all the rest of the
          shit in your life for a few hours…

                    CANTONA
          I'm glad you remember…

                    ERIC
          I miss the games…only place you can let rip
          without being arrested…shout…scream…
          laugh…

                    CANTONA
          Even cry…and see Englishmen kiss…

                    ERIC
          Where else can you sing? [Pause] Right…
          sweetest moment ever?

Cantona smiles to himself.

                    CANTONA
          Sweetest…[thinking] It wasn't a goal…

ERIC

Must have been!…Last minute…Cup final
against Liverpool?…Victory away to
Newcastle…caught them and won the
league…It's got to be a goal Eric.

Cantona shakes his head.

CANTONA

No…it was a pass…

Eric thinks. A moment of realisation. His face comes to light.

ERIC

My God…to Giggs against Leeds!

More roars from a crowd…

FADE TO FLASHBACK OF THE PASS AND GOAL

CANTONA

I knew how fast he was…his good side…it
came in a flash…just flicked it with the outside
of my boot…surprised everyone…He took it
in his stride and my heart soared…

ERIC

A gift…

CANTONA

Like an offering…to the Great God of
Football…

ERIC

And if he had missed?

CANTONA

> You have to trust your teammates...always. If
> not...we are lost.

A moment between them.

ERIC

> Must have been tough after you were
> banned...nine months! Bastards...

FLASHBACK – REAL NEWS FOOTAGE:

Cantona does his karate kick. 'He's in deep trouble now.'

Media circus on his way to court. Journalists hound him, and
even a line from John Major.

Cantona runs round an empty pitch absolutely alone.

CANTONA

> I hard to work hard...dig deep inside. I
> needed something to fill me up when I was on
> my own...something to aim for...

ERIC

> Funny...sometimes we forget you are just a
> man...

Cantona turns to look at him. Deadly serious.

CANTONA

> I am not a man...I am [pause] 'Cantona'.

A moment between them. Eric realises he's taking the piss and
both burst out laughing.

ERIC

> But what did you do to keep yourself going?

Pause.

> CANTONA
>
> I learn the trumpet.

They both laugh.

> ERIC
>
> Trumpet!…[shaking his head] having me on
> Eric…

Cantona, with a twinkle in his eye, grabs his holdall. Eric is stunned to see Cantona pull out a trumpet, put it to his lips, and very very badly, but recognisably, all fingers and thumbs, begin to play the Marseillaise.

Eric laughs at Cantona's red puffed-out face.

Sudden sound of door being snapped open.

An old woman suspiciously stares down at the lone figure of Eric on the steps in front of her.

> WOMAN
>
> What's wrong with you? Muttering away like
> a pervert! Are you on strike?

21. ANOTHER STREET

Eric, now by himself, pulls his trolley behind and makes his deliveries in a street of substantial houses with ornamental gardens.

He opens a gate to a large house with long drive.

Halfway up he is intrigued by two workmen who are in the process of installing three mythological mock Greek statues in the garden.

ERIC

Very nice…all the way from Ancient Greece?

The workmen laugh. A black Mercedes pulls into the drive and sweeps past them towards the house.

WORKMAN 1

Ancient Sweden…looks like Ikea…

WORKMAN 2

…think it was Homer it said on the package…

ERIC

Homer Simpson?…Does it flash at night and do break dance?

The workmen chuckle as they dig round the base of the statue.

Eric turns towards the house and notices the same man [Zac] who slapped Ryan staring at him from beside his car. He has another tough-looking associate with him, FENNER. It stops Eric in his tracks.

ZAC

Something amusing you want to share?

Eric and Zac notice Fenner recording them on his mobile.

ERIC

No…just admiring the artwork…

ZAC

What do you like about it?

ERIC

Well…[struggling] just a nice shape…

ZAC

'Nice shape...' See the shape of you run you
skinny prick...

Zac opens the door of his car and a vicious pit bull skips out.

ZAC (CONT'D)
Go get him boy!

ERIC
Fuck!!

Eric drops his trolley and runs like hell as the pit bull takes
after him.

Eric scrambles through the gate and by a whisker slams the
gate shut as the beast jumps furiously behind the bars.

Eric is stunned as he stares at its slobbering gums pulled back
over terrifying teeth.

Eric looks up at Zac now pulling the post trolley towards him
accompanied by Fenner who still records on the mobile. Both
are greatly amused and Zac plays up to the mobile recording.
Performing.

ZAC
World record by a postman...

FENNER
0 – 60 in 2.3 seconds...How are your pants?

ERIC
Can I have the trolley back please?

ZAC
Did you swear at my dog?

ERIC

Just got a fright…

FENNER

Apologise…

ERIC

Don't want any trouble…

ZAC

Apologise!

ERIC

I'm sorry…

ZAC

Not to me…[pointing at the dog] to Winston.

Fenner chuckles loudly as he steps closer with the phone.

Winston senses the aggression and growls even more. Eric hesitates. Zac puts his hand on the gate.

ZAC (CONT'D)

If I open this…he'll tear your sausage off.

ERIC

I'm sorry…Winston.

ZAC

'Mr' Winston.

ERIC

I'm sorry Mr Winston.

Zac hurls Eric's post trolley over the gate.

The two men are greatly entertained and head up the driveway as the two shocked workmen stare, and then go back to work.

Fenner is already examining his artwork on the mobile.

Pale and shaken Eric picks up his trolley and walks off.

22. ERIC'S HOUSE

Eric, wearing an apron, cooks the evening meal.

In mid-manoeuvre he hears the doorbell ring.

He opens the door and he is amazed to find Lily staring at him with Daisy on one arm, a folding pram on the other.

> LILY
> Sorry Eric…your mobile's off…My mother
> tripped on the step…hurt her ribs…can you
> take Daisy and I'll take her to Emergency in
> case she's cracked something…can I come in?

Eric, still stunned, nods.

Lily steps inside. Eric takes the pram and then sudden panic as he sees Lily head for the front room.

> ERIC
> No Lily! You can't go in there!…It's filthy…
> Stop!

He scrambles up, but it is too late. Lily is in the sitting room which is in its usual chaotic state. Her eyes scan a pitiful sight.

> LILY
> So your butler's away Eric? What do you call
> that killer disease again…Ebola? Better get out
> of here…[pause, as she spots something] while
> we can…

She hands Daisy to Eric and then moves over to the mantelpiece.

LILY (CONT'D)

[To herself] Oh my God…

She has her hand on her mouth. She stares at a very distinctive Picasso postcard, tastefully framed, and standing on the mantelpiece beside a coloured candle.

LILY (CONT'D)

[Still half to herself] It can't be…

Eric stares at the postcard in total amazement.

She stretches out her hand, picks it up. Hesitating, she turns it round. It has no back and she can read her own writing. She holds it to her chest.

She looks up at Eric. Her eyes fill, and she turns away to hide. She lays it back down on the mantelpiece and then sits on the corner of a seat as she tries to regain her composure.

Eric has no idea what to do. His eyes jump between Lily and the card.

LILY

[She almost chokes] I'm sorry…[pause, then she pulls herself together].We should never have agreed to do this…Sam will have to find someone else…

Lily shoots out of the room and runs off.

Eric is still rooted to the spot. He moves over to the card, and turns it round to look at her writing. Still dumbfounded.

ERIC

[Shouting] Jess…

Jess pokes his head round the corner. Eric pops Daisy into his arms and rushes back to the window to see Lily take off in her car.

ERIC

Jesus…

[Perhaps the faintest sound of a distant trumpet.]

Eric's mind races. He rushes over to the door of the sitting room.

ERIC

Where did Ryan park the car?

JESS

Not back yet…

ERIC

Shit! Where's your bike?

JESS

Round the back…

Eric sprints off.

ERIC

Look after Daisy for me…

JESS

Don't know what to do…

ERIC

You'll learn…

23. STREETS: LILY'S HOUSE

VARIOUS STREETS: Eric cycles like a mad man. [Sense of changing from a tough area to a more peaceful one.]

He causes panic at traffic lights as he skips through red.

He looks like he's going to have a heart-attack as he cycles up a hill.

ANOTHER STREET: the houses are very different. He cycles downhill at speed and skids to a stop at a familiar car. Lily's.

He stares at a tidy little house with manicured garden, and feels his nerve begin to desert him.

He jumps off the bike and drops it on the pavement.

He hesitates for a second and then walks up to the door and rings the bell.

He can see a light on upstairs. No answer.

He rings the bell again. Still no answer.

He looks through the letter box and sees a shadow in the kitchen. He shouts through the letter box.

ERIC
I know you're in there Lily…I need to speak
to you…

He rings the doorbell again.

ERIC (CONT'D)
[Again through the letter box] Please Lily…
just two minutes…is that too much to ask? I'll
never bother you again…

He knocks the door with his knuckles.

Silence. Still no answer. He walks down the steps into the garden. He hears the lock turn in the door.

He turns round to see the door open, but with the chain on. Lily's face is half hidden in the dark behind the six-inch gap.

Eric tentatively approaches.

ERIC (CONT'D)

Is your mum okay?

Lily tries to hide that she has been crying.

LILY

My brother took her to the hospital…she'll be fine…just bruising…Stop looking at me!

ERIC

Lily…[long pause] I just wanted to try and…[looking for the word] explain…

LILY

[Incredulous] 'Explain'…explain…What planet are you on?

ERIC

I'm sorry Lily…

LILY

Sorry…I was just twenty-one Eric! I had your baby…I loved you to pieces…You walked out on me…never came back…You left me to raise a child on my own…Oh my God…and you want to 'explain'…I'm a grandmother for Christ's sake! Have you totally flipped?! Would you like me to 'explain' how many nights I cried myself to sleep? How I fell apart? How I had to build my whole life again? [More to herself] Shit! Shit! Why am I telling you this?! Did it ever occur to you to listen first you selfish useless prick?!

Eric hangs his head in shame.

ERIC

You're right...

LILY

Don't fucking agree with me!! You've no right! How dare you leave that card there and invite me in like that...Get out of my sight!

Lily takes a deep breath and tries to calm herself.

LILY (CONT'D)

Ah Jesus...what am I saying...Go away Eric Bishop...I just don't care.

She slams the door. Eric stares at it for a few moments and then wanders back to his bike.

With a wobble, he heads off up the hill.

24. ERIC'S ROOM

Eric and Cantona share another spliff. Cantona has that same twinkle in his eye.

CANTONA

Très bien...she hates you! Now we go somewhere!

ERIC

We're going nowhere! She's right...I've totally flipped...We're both fucking grandparents...

111

Cantona thinks for a moment, and then, in some style, comes out with another proverb in French.

                    ERIC (CONT'D)
          I wish you'd stop this bullshit!

                    CANTONA
          Okay...I don't translate...

Eric looks at him for several long moments as he struggles with his curiosity. Cantona enjoys the moment.

                    ERIC
          Fuck it...what does it mean?

                    CANTONA
          No...I will not be a burden...

                    ERIC
          Tell me...

                    CANTONA
          No...we French have good manners...

                    ERIC
          Come on Eric!

Pause.

                    CANTONA
          'The noblest vengeance...[pause] is to forgive'.

Eric ponders on the words. Silence for a few moments as he struggles and his eyebrows furrow.

                    ERIC
          She might forgive me?

His mobile bleeps with a message.

Eric checks it.

ERIC (CONT'D)

Shit…It's Lily.

Eric hesitates, but gains strength from Cantona.

ERIC (CONT'D)

[Reading] 'Meet me in the pub…you know
which one. Now.' [To Cantona] Fuck…

Cantona smiles.

25. OLD PUB IN MANCHESTER

Tiny cramped pub with odd shape.

Lily sits in a snug corner covered with hundreds of
photographs and memorabilia. There are old photographs from
the sixties all the way through to the present and includes one
of a young Eric Cantona. Her eyes glance around the walls,
and then to Eric buying the drinks at a tiny little bar that
hasn't changed since they were last there.

The whole atmosphere gets to her. Eric, still nervous and wary,
lays down the drinks.

LILY

[Almost a whisper, looking around] It feels like
yesterday…

ERIC

[Glancing round] It's hardly changed…

LILY

But we have.

There is a moment between them as Eric takes a drink for
courage. She holds his eye.

                            ERIC

I'm really scared to open all this up...

                            LILY

I don't care...

Eric takes a deep breath to try and calm himself.

                            ERIC

I've bottled out so many times...[He looks at
her. Long pause] It happened the first time at
Sam's christening party...remember?

She nods.

                       ERIC (CONT'D)

At first I thought it was just too hot and
smoky...too many bodies in one room...all the
handshakes...slaps on the back...corny jokes...
all the advice about a new baby...What are
your plans now son? Different ball game now
son...They went on and on...one after another
...my old man kept staring across at me...that
crabbit scowl of his...he was beside Uncle
Michael who looked like death...remember
him? In and out of the asylum.

Lily nods.

26. FLASHBACK: BAR AT SMALL CRICKET CLUB

A smoky cramped room full of Eric's and Lily's family and
friends. A young Eric, dressed in suit and tie, is surrounded by
relatives in the process of getting pissed. In the far corner Lily
and the new baby are the centre of attention. At some point
Lily may breastfeed the baby. Eric pulls at his tie,
uncomfortable in the press of people and congratulations.

                            114

ERIC VOICE OVER

…Aunt Mary came up…yap yap yapping…
how to save money…routine in a child's
life…how important this how important that…
just wouldn't shut up…and then she started on
about that bloody washing machine she bought
us…remember? As if she was reading the
fucking entire instructions! [Lily smiles, pause]
Daft Lily…but I felt my tie getting tighter…
my clothes shrinking…my heart thumping…
and then my father came up to me…no
backslapping from him…just those hard little
eyes and clipped tongue of his…

BACK TO THE PUB:

LILY

Yeah…remember the night we went round and
we told him I was pregnant?

Eric rolls his eyes at the memory.

ERIC

As he came up I caught your eye…you were
feeding Sam in the corner…you blew me a
kiss…for some reason it drove him mad…he
started prodding me…the way he always did
as a child…on the ribs with that stubby short
finger of his…'Fucking kisses!…See how long
that lasts…You had the brains to go to college
…now we'll see what you're made of…made
your bed now son…lie on it!' Felt as if my
head was inside a plastic bag…

FLASHBACK:

A severe looking man, JACK BISHOP, is lecturing Eric. He shouts in his ear to be heard above the noise.

Eric's distress accelerates. Something hard and mechanical about his father.

> ERIC VOICE OVER
> …Snapping to and fro…his voice louder and louder…'Made your bed now son…made your bed now son…' On and on and on! His prods in the chest…I started to choke and then I caught sight of you and Sam again through the bodies…then Uncle Michael just sitting there…rocking…And that's when it happened. [Pause] You won't understand Lily…[struggling to find the words]…felt as if I just floated off…out of my own body…I was up there stuck to the fucking ceiling…looking down on myself…Eric Bishop with Jack Bishop… ironmonger…poking my chest in slow motion…'Fucking kisses!…Made your bed now son…made your bed now son.'

BACK TO THE PUB:

> ERIC
> I was terrified! I couldn't breathe… panicked…stumbled through everybody…I just ran and ran…and sobbed and sobbed…I couldn't stop…

Eye to eye for a moment.

LILY

It was a panic attack…more common than you
think…we come across it in the clinic all the
time…

ERIC

I didn't know…[Pause] After half an hour I
calmed down…came back…put on an act…
[Long moment] Been doing it ever since.

Long pause.

LILY

Why didn't you tell me?

ERIC

Blanked it out…even to myself…I was
terrified…I thought I was going nuts like
Uncle Michael…

LILY

Did it happen again?

Eric nods. Long pause. She can see Eric struggle but holds his
eye.

ERIC

My days off…those were the worst…that tiny
flat…smell of the new paint…that big pram
that took up the entire hall…Your mam there
every day…she was so good I felt useless…

He takes another sip of his drink.

ERIC (CONT'D)

You won't believe this Lily…One morning I
was up at six with Sam. I put on a wash…that

rumble…mesmerised me…and then! [pause]…
there on the glass door of Aunt Mary's
spanking new fucking washing machine…
among the nappies…my old man's face
appeared. [Lily, though shocked, can't help but
let out a nervous laugh at the image]…
'Fucking kisses…Made your bed now son…
made your bed now son.' Again and again…
Fuck! I really thought I was cracking up…
imagined myself like Uncle Michael…in the
blood…that's how it started…[Pause] Later I'd
see you feeding Sam…I can't explain it but I
just couldn't handle it…I began to get scared
of going home…

Pause.

LILY

But why couldn't you tell me?

ERIC

Oh yeah…just seen my old man again inside
the washing machine…can't keep the fucker
out!

She half laughs into herself. Another moment between them.

LILY

Thought you'd gone all cold…regretted the
baby…[Pause] I just wanted you to touch
me…I felt so fat and ugly…clothes always
stinking of milk…hardly slept…[Pause] I had a
good go at you didn't I? [He nods sheepishly] I
didn't know I could scream like that…

ERIC

Don't blame you...staying out...getting
drunk...off with the boys...the excuses...you
thought I was with that girl from the bar but it
wasn't till after I left you...

LILY

All the lies you told...felt so lonely...you fell
asleep in the couch once after a night out. I
saw a love bite on your neck...felt so betrayed
...I remember I wanted to stab you right
through it...something just came over me...I
could have done it.

Pause.

ERIC

I remember the morning I left you Lily...
early shift...4.30. You'd fallen asleep with the
watch strap still in your hand...timing the
feeds. Sam was twitching...little noises...She
woke up and looked right at me. I felt the
room begin to spin...the plastic bag again...
my old man's finger...'made your bed now
son'. You're not going to believe this Lily...not
so much I left you...which I did...I just
couldn't get back.

He turns away. Long long moment between them.

LILY

Why are you telling me now...after all this
time?

ERIC

Last week Lily…when I was supposed to meet
you…I flipped again.

Another long pause. Lily fidgets with her drink.

LILY

We were so young…almost kids.

27. A TOW PATH BY THE CANAL

Eric walks home by a canal after saying goodbye to Lily.

He stops for a moment by the water.

He stares into the depths, thinking.

On the opposite side two young lovers kiss passionately and
unselfconsciously on a park bench.

28. SORTING OFFICE

Eric, at his usual spot by the corner, sorts his mail into the
thirty-odd boxes in front of him. While not at top speed he's
looking much better. Monk and Meatballs watch him from the
distance. Both are impressed.

MEATBALLS

Must have been the Dalai Lama…

MONK

I suspect hormones…the old ying and yang.

29. MANCHESTER STREET

Three buses fill up with FC United Supporters on a match day.

There is a great atmosphere, and Eric, watching it all with Daisy in pram, is warmly greeted by several old mates one after another. Many bend down to talk to Daisy who is wide eyed at the action.

The buses almost bounce with the songs and chants from inside.

> FAN 1
>
> Hey Eric!…Good to see you man…are you coming?

> ERIC
>
> Another day…good to see you too…

Meatballs and Spleen scoot around, latter as frenetic as ever, and try to get a gang of lively young supporters on the bus.

> SPLEEN
>
> New blood Eric…[punching the air] We shall overcome!

Meatballs comes over to him.

> MEATBALLS
>
> Come on with us…bring Daisy…no problem …she'll love it!

> ERIC
>
> No…meeting Lily.

Meatballs' eyes light up.

MEATBALLS

That's great Eric…I loved that girl…she was
special. [Pause] Are you getting back together
again?

ERIC

No! Just chat when we pass the baby back and
forward…Jesus Christ man…

MEATBALLS

That's good…

FAN 1

Come on Meatballs! Move it!

Eric laughs and waves at more old faces as the buses pull out
and the chants continue.

30. A CAFE

Eric and Lily, in the middle of a conversation, have another
coffee as Daisy sleeps.

LILY

But Chrissie had two boys…different
fathers…did you not feel overwhelmed?

ERIC

They weren't mine…one wasn't even hers…
Didn't feel the same weight…I was going to
help…play my part…but they weren't mine…
If I'm honest in the back of my mind I was
getting ready to run again…Chrissie wanted
another child…I took all the weight…even
before she started drinking…I got really close
to them…[pause] loved them…we had a lot of

122

fun…their fathers didn't give a shit…then
when Chrissie ran off they wanted to stay with
me…suited her fine…she was really lost.
[Pause] We both were…manic most of the
time…filling up the days and nights so we
didn't have to talk…

Long pause. Lily watches him as he struggles to come to terms
with it.

ERIC (CONT'D)

I really really tried with the boys…when they
got older I fucked it up…

LILY

Not easy…teenage years…

ERIC

They've turned into selfish bastards…

LILY

You brought them up…

Eric stops for a moment and looks at her.

ERIC

Yeah…it's me Lily…pathetic…I'm like a
fucking doormat…can't stop them wiping
their boots in my face…

LILY

Yes you can. [Pause] A lot of people wouldn't
have bothered…not your kids.

ERIC

[Sharp, deadly serious] Yes they are. [Pause, it
takes her aback] The day Chrissie walked

out…[a moment between them] I promised
them both I'd look after them, no matter
what. [Pause] Maybe I was trying to make up
for Sam…

Another long moment between them.

31. OUTSIDE THE LIBRARY – 10PM

Eric and Lily, sitting on a bench, with Daisy asleep in the
pram, wait for Sam outside the library.

A few dozen students stream out carrying their books.

They spot Sam, one of the last to leave. She is carrying a huge
pile of books in her bag. She stops to chat in animated fashion
to a couple of friends. She's laughing.

> ERIC
> I'll always be grateful you never turned her
> against me…

Lily looks at her hands.

> LILY
> I'll be honest…it really hurt me she had so
> much fun with you…it didn't seem fair…

> ERIC
> You got all the crap…homework…complaints
> …I brought her to see Cantona…

> LILY
> Yes…and no…[Without rancour] You know
> something…I was so furious with you…but
> sometimes I couldn't help thinking…'My
> God…what that man is missing…' She was a
> precious child…she really pulled me through…

hard work but she was so much fun…and
despite myself…I could see you in her
sometimes…that got me when I was down…it
was a waste such a gorgeous child didn't have
someone else to enjoy her as much as me…You
missed so much Eric.

A moment between them.

Sam scurries down the steps and then checks her mobile. Lily
and Eric smile at each other.

She is about to pass them.

ERIC

Sam!

She stops dead in her tracks. She stares at Eric and Lily side by
side with the pram beside them.

She rushes over.

SAM

Jesus…something wrong with Daisy?

LILY

Nothing…sleeping like an angel.

Sam is still stunned. Silence, as her eyes flick between the two
of them.

SAM

My God…[touched] Have you been…talking?

Eric and Lily turn to look at each other.

They both shake their heads.

Lily takes Eric's arm. He visibly freezes. Lily lets go.

32. ERIC'S HOUSE – NIGHT

Eric and Cantona are in the middle of a discussion.

> CANTONA
>
> It's like riding a bike…kicking a ball…always
> with you…

> ERIC
>
> Lost it…all gone…I'm serious…

> CANTONA
>
> Nobody forgets rock and roll!

> ERIC
>
> I have…

That look again from Cantona. He shakes his head.

> CANTONA
>
> What's wrong?

Eric sinks into himself.

> ERIC
>
> I haven't touched anyone…in years…I just
> can't do it…she took my arm…fuck! I just
> froze…just talking about it makes me panic!
> [Deep breath] Come…let's talk about
> football…

Cantona stares at him for a moment and then leaps from the
couch. At speed he kicks off his shoes, rolls up his trousers to
reveal powerful hairy calves as Eric begins to panic. Cantona
grabs a bright red towel, wraps it round his waist, opens the
four top buttons of his shirt, wraps the collar inside as if it was
a blouse [revealing more hair on his chest] and stares at Eric.

CANTONA

> I'm the girl.

He points at the music centre with his finger. As if by magic we hear...

ELVIS

> 'One for the money, two for the show...'

Cantona grabs Eric and pulls him up to rock and roll.

They both go for it – no prizes but certainly full marks for effort.

DOWNSTAIRS:

Jess, in some alarm, runs into Ryan's room, immediately below Eric's.

They both stare at the pounding ceiling as if it's about to collapse.

There is an almighty bounce and then thundering crash.

Above the rock and roll they can hear Eric hoot in laughter. They turn to each other in amazement.

RYAN

> Is he laughing?

BACK TO ERIC'S ROOM:

Eric rolls about in helpless laughter at Cantona's efforts to play the girl.

Eric tries to twirl Cantona but it ends up a mess.

But Cantona keeps at it, twisting and turning and shaking his arse like a real hot chick.

The music ends.

Both are breathless. Cantona whips off the towel, wipes his brow, and winks at him.

CANTONA

Want to fuck?

ERIC

Jesus!

LATER: Eric and Cantona share another generous spliff.

CANTONA

[With deep inhalation] Women…women…
[deeper draw yet] Women! [French, without
translating] 'Woman is the confusion of man'…

He hands the spliff to Eric.

ERIC

She works part time so she can help her
mum…help Sam…baby massage…old folks
home she does the same…nourishes everything
she touches…'But I need time for myself
Eric'…that's what she said…

FLASHBACK:THE CAFE

LILY

I've chosen a simple life Eric…but it's mine. I
need time for myself…I'd rather have more
time than more things. I gave up a safe boring
job…retrained to do physio…I do what I
love…you forced me to change. [Long pause]
Everything I imagined just crumbled…I never
expected to be on my own…

She pauses to pull herself together.

> LILY (CONT'D)
> …Remember the Leonard Cohen song?…
> 'There's a crack, a crack in everything, [Eric
> nods] That's where the light comes in'. I had to
> find out who I was…not easy by yourself with
> a toddler.

Eric's head goes down in shame.

ERIC'S ROOM:

Cantona just listens.

> ERIC
> 'I want to make my life more beautiful
> Eric'…that's what she said…'simple daily
> things'…she makes lovely meals…wears nice
> clothes she makes herself…meets friends that
> do her good…[lighting up] Know what she
> does…once every three months she picks out a
> little bed and breakfast on the net…near a
> river…a lovely walk…by the sea…or an old
> church…

FLASHBACK: THE CAFE

> LILY
> I just up and go…never to the same place…an
> adventure…I need to build in little surprises
> Eric…

Eric hesitates, wondering whether or not he should ask the
question.

ERIC

Wao…do you not get lonely?

LILY

No…sometimes I take a lover.

Eric chokes on his tea and is totally embarrassed by his coughing and spluttering. At last he recovers.

ERIC

Jesus…think that went down the wrong way…

Lily grins.

LILY

Yeah…I think it did.

Eric, still trying to recover as he wipes up his spilt tea and empties the flooded saucer. Embarrassed he looks up at her.

LILY (CONT'D)

I went through hell Eric. [Pause] Never again.
I've got my health…lots to live for…I'm going
to enjoy it.

She glances at her watch and calls over the waiter for the bill.

LILY (CONT'D)

Ah…nearly forgot!

She bends down and grabs a battered and dusty old brown bag from under the pram.

LILY (CONT'D)

These are yours…

Eric takes it and opens up the bag to reveal an old pair of pointed blue suede shoes.

ERIC

[Smiling] Jesus Christ…can't believe it…

LILY

One night I made a bonfire in the back
garden…I got every single thing that belonged
to you…then I came to these…I tried to throw
them on…just couldn't do it…

A long moment between them.

ERIC

It was a good night…

He looks up and they hold eyes for a moment.

LILY

Have you got someone you can speak to?

Eric hesitates.

ERIC

Sort of…

LILY

Good…

BACK TO ERIC'S ROOM:

Cantona nods.

CANTONA

I like this woman! [French] She has balls! Big
balls!

ERIC

[Determined] One day she's going to look me
in the eye and not feel sorry for me…that's all
I want.

CANTONA

A personal trainer! New regime! Day one!

33. PARK

Eric, wearing an old Man United top, with Cantona's name printed on the back, and shorts that are a bit too tight, does his best to do 'Knees up' exercises.

Cantona's knees pound like pistons, as Eric looks next door to a heart-attack.

CANTONA (CONT'D)

Higher! Faster! After you throw up a few times…you feel fantastique…

Monk and Jack stand behind a fence that looks down on the park. They stare at a solitary Eric. He is now skipping and punching his arms in the air. They study Eric at his athletic best.

JACK

What the fuck…is that Eric?

MONK

He's getting worse. Phone Meatballs!

JACK

No…he'll have us meditating in our Y-fronts…

Eric, passing in front of them, switches to a professional footballer's exercise – criss-crossed steps at speed running sideways. They are amazed. He falls on his arse. He sees them laughing.

ERIC

Don't fucking laugh. This is a changed man. I
want you round at my place. Seven o'clock
tonight.

34. ERIC'S HOUSE

Ryan, Jess, and three of their mates lie about in the sitting
room watching a porn DVD.

There is a noise outside.

They sit up in their seats, alert.

The door opens. Meatballs bursts in with Jack, Spleen and Eric
behind them.

MEATBALLS

How are you boys?

The boys are stunned as the four men watch the action from
the side as the boys begin to squirm on the couch.

On screen the artistes now perform a threesome, with bodies
and bits contorted all over the place.

MEATBALLS (CONT'D)

I never knew you could do that…is that
allowed?

SPLEEN

Don't knock it till you've tried it…eh boys?

Dark expressionless faces fixed to the spot.

More huffing and puffing…and at last, satisfaction.

JACK

So there is a better job than a postman's…

Meatballs and Spleen disconnect the TV in a flash.

The boys are stunned as Meatballs and Spleen carry it out.

> ERIC
>
> There's another one in the kitchen and three
> upstairs…

Their faces drop.

> RYAN
>
> What the fuck do you think you are playing
> at?

> JACK
>
> You should get a few bob for these Eric…

> ERIC
>
> See you later boys. Tidy up eh?

35. KITCHEN – LATER

Eric, at the bench, finishes laying out the food on a plate.

The smell of food has Jess scurrying to the kitchen.

Ryan is not far behind.

Eric flips a delicious steak and fried onions onto a plate. He then adds in a few veg, plus freshly fried chips.

The boys settle down to eat.

Eric grabs his piled-up plate and settles down at the opposite end of the table to the boys.

They stare at Eric, at each other and flick their eyes over to the cooker. Jess peers over and realises there is nothing left. He shakes his head at Ryan.

ERIC (CONT'D)

Can you pass down the salt?

They glance at each other. Jess passes it down to him.

Eric digs into his grub. He enjoys each morsel more than he can remember.

RYAN

Think this will make a difference...eh?

Eric shrugs.

ERIC

Doubt it...but it makes me feel so much better...

RYAN

You haven't got a clue what's going on...not a clue.

Ryan jumps out. The door slams viciously behind him.

JESS

Pushed you too far...eh?

Eric nods.

ERIC

Treated me like shit...No more.

There is a moment between them.

Eric gets up and moves to the fridge for a drink. Jess stares at the plate as Eric continues to rustle in the fridge.

Jess, in a flash, grabs Eric's plate and runs for the door.

ERIC (CONT'D)

Come here you little bastard!

Jess scrambles up the first flight of stairs to the toilet, and slams the door shut, and locks it, as Eric gives chase.

From inside the toilet.

> JESS
> Eric…this is the best grub you've ever made…Ahhhh…delicious…do you want a chip?

He pokes a chip under the door.

Eric starts laughing. It surprises them both.

> JESS (CONT'D)
> This is so good…I might even wash the dishes…

Eric, at the door, smiles to himself.

36. ERIC'S ROOM – NIGHT

Eric sits on his seat thinking.

He stares at the phone, and hesitates. He stares up at Cantona's poster. It seems to give him heart.

He picks up the phone and dials. It rings out twice but then he panics and puts it down.

He prowls round the room.

Now his phone starts ringing. He hesitates and then picks it up.

> LILY'S VOICE
> Eric…did you just phone me?

He winces.

ERIC

Yeah...It was me Lily.

LILY

And?

ERIC

Christ...I forgot what I was going to ask
you...

LILY

So you put the phone down?

Silence.

ERIC

Do you want to come round for a bite to eat
at the weekend...Sam can join us when she's
finished...only if you feel like it...and you
have nothing else on...and you're not shagging
some hairy lover in a bed and breakfast in the
lake district...

Silence.

LILY

Yes Eric...I'd like that.

Silence.

LILY (CONT'D)

I'm vegetarian now.

ERIC

Vegetarian? I'll do boiled organic parsnips...
with chips...

Daisy starts crying by her side.

LILY
Got to go…thanks Eric.

Eric puts down the phone and jumps up. Animated. He nods at the Cantona poster and with fingers to his lips, signs the inhalation of a joint.

ERIC
[Imitating Cantona's accent] A puuff?

He goes to the door.

RYAN'S ROOM:

Eric moves in tentatively, bends down and rolls up the Man U rug. He unpicks the loose wooden floorboard. By the hash is a red coloured cloth.

Curious, he picks it up and is surprised by its weight. He unravels the cloth and reveals a thick handgun.

He is absolutely stunned. He stands up and just stares at the squat beast in his hand.

ERIC (CONT'D)
Fuck…

He marches into Jess's room.

Jess is half asleep.

ERIC (CONT'D)
Did you know about this?

Jess stares in amazement.

ERIC (CONT'D)
Tell me the truth Jess! I really mean it!

JESS

Honestly…I know nothing about it…

Eric sinks onto Jess's bed.

ERIC

Ahh Christ…what the fuck is going on in my
own home…

Eric is beside himself.

ERIC (CONT'D)

He can't be using it…is he?

JESS

I don't know…maybe it's a fake…

ERIC

This is disgusting! [Thinking] That ponce in
the black fucking car…

Jess hesitates.

ERIC (CONT'D)

Who the hell is he Jess?

JESS

Zac…got a big crew behind him…a real hard
case and done time…He's clever…but fucking
mad…he's got Ryan [clenching his fist] like
that…I tried to warn him but he told me to
piss off…everybody's so scared of him…

ERIC

When did all this start? Why didn't you tell
me?

Jess looks away.

                              JESS
        I tried to Eric...but...

                              ERIC
        [Snapping] But what?

                              JESS
        You didn't seem to care...

Eric sighs into himself. He stares down at the gun again.

                              ERIC
        Fuck...

Jess looks disturbed too.

                        ERIC (CONT'D)
        Where is he?...Do you know?

Jess shakes his head.

                        ERIC (CONT'D)
        You've got to help me...

39. ERIC'S HOUSE – LATER

Eric, with the gun in his hand, prowls by the window.

Eric hears a powerful motorbike pull up. He looks out.

The rider stays put, while Ryan, on the passenger seat, skips into the house.

Eric can hear him enter and run up the stairs to his room.

Eric sneaks down.

He moves closer to Ryan's room and peeks round the corner at him as he unpicks the loose floorboard.

Ryan feels around desperately for the missing gun.

> RYAN
>
> Fuck!

> ERIC
>
> Looking for this?

Ryan springs up and confronts him as Eric holds the gun behind his back.

> RYAN
>
> Give me it Eric…just give me the thing and
> mind your own business…

> ERIC
>
> Thing! It's a gun Ryan for fuck's sake.

Ryan pleads desperately.

> RYAN
>
> Please give me it Eric…you don't know what's
> going on

> ERIC
>
> You better tell me…

There is a loud whistle from outside from a motorbike rider. Ryan runs to the window.

His desperation turns to anger. Jess, half asleep, bursts into the room.

> RYAN
>
> Give me it now or I'm in the shit…all of us!

> ERIC
>
> Tell him to fuck off…[moving to the window]
> I will then…

RYAN

Oh God…

Ryan takes a mad rush at Eric, throws him up against the wall.
The gun drops. Eric tries to push back.

JESS

Stop it…both of you!

Eric grabs onto Ryan's jacket and won't let go.

RYAN

Eric let go…you've got to let me go…

ERIC

No way!

Ryan snaps. He punches Eric full force in the face which sends
him flying against the wall. His face is covered in blood.

Ryan bends down quickly, and snaps up the gun.

Eric flings himself at Ryan's leg and grabs an ankle.

RYAN

I'm warning you…fuck off!

JESS

Stop it! Stop it!

ERIC

I'm not letting you go Ryan…

Ryan struggles like mad to get free. He has to stamp and kick
like a mad thing. Still Eric hangs on.

Ryan pounds at Eric's arm still round his leg.

RYAN

Silly old prick! Fuck off!

At last he breaks free and sprints down the stairs with the gun. Jess, really upset, sinks down against the wall.

He has tears in his eyes as he sees Eric struggle up.

He moves over and helps him onto the bed.

Jess is really upset.

JESS

I can't believe this…

38. VARIOUS STREETS – SAME NIGHT

Eric, with a badly swollen face, drives his old car around various spots of Manchester with Jess beside him. Jess examines his mobile as one text after another comes in.

A – OUTSIDE A NIGHTCLUB:

Eric pulls up by a nightclub, but doesn't cut the engine. A dozen young people spill out into the street. Nearly all of them are blind drunk. A couple of boys throw traffic cones at each other, while a group of girls, in the skimpiest of shorts, high heels, and light blouses, curse them from the pavement.

One falls over and two others struggle to pull her up. Instead, they collapse in a pile.

Another text comes to Jess's phone.

JESS

Nothing…nobody's seen him.

ERIC

Shit!

                              JESS
        Sometimes he hangs around with the
        bouncers...

                              ERIC
        What bouncers?

                              JESS
        For the nightclubs...if you control the door...
        control the club...or the taxi office...all Zac's
        mates...

                              ERIC
        How many pies has this bastard got his paws
        in?

B – OUTSIDE OFFICE:

Eric drives down a sidestreet and stops outside a run-down
office with faded paint.

Five big beefy guys stand outside chatting and looking around
them. They are tough and aggressive, and very aware of what is
going on around them.

Eric parks opposite them. Jess runs over to them. Brief
exchange.

Jess returns.

                              JESS
        Haven't seen him...or so they say.

Eric continues to examine the men opposite as they stare at
him. They seem to be taking the piss at the state of the car
[signing for steering wheel and mock admiration with a
thumbs up]. One of them is already on a mobile.

ERIC

I didn't know he was hanging around with
guys like that...Is he writing down my
number plate?

JESS

Lots you don't know Eric...

They pull off.

C – OUTSIDE A TAXI FIRM – LATER:

As Eric turns into a sidestreet a taxi screeches to a halt outside
a taxi office close by. A half dozen drivers, congregated on the
street, sprint towards a driver who has just arrived. He gives
them some urgent news. Shouts between them. One is now on
a mobile.

A police siren screeches in the distance.

ERIC

What the fuck is going on?

Eric pulls to a halt by them as Jess skips out. More sirens and
animated exchanges.

Suddenly Jess starts running to Eric.

JESS

Somebody's been shot outside the pool club...

ERIC

My God...who?

JESS

They don't know...one of the drivers went
past...Police everywhere...armed boys too...

                    ERIC
He's not shot someone…or hurt himself…

                    JESS
He's got a bulletproof vest…

                    ERIC
What?!

                    JESS
I thought you saw it…when you were
fighting…

                    ERIC
Jesus Christ! What's going on…

He accelerates off.

D – BY THE POOL CLUB:

Eric drives by the pool club.

A flashing ambulance is there too, surrounded by several police
cars and a police van which is double parked.

A half dozen policemen are in the process of putting up a
cordon.

A frustrated policeman waves Eric on as he slows and tries to
peer inside.

Another siren howls in the distance.

39. SITTING ROOM – ERIC'S HOUSE – MORNING

Eric, sitting by himself, hears a click at the front door.

Footsteps. He looks up.

Ryan stands at the door and stares at him.

He moves in and sits down on a chair opposite. He looks in a bad state. He puts his hand into his pocket and tosses a gun onto the table which crashes down loudly. He takes off his jacket, his top, and then pulls off a bulletproof vest which he slings down too.

RYAN

Don't know what to do...

ERIC

You shot someone...

RYAN

No Eric! First he told me it was just a fake...
then only to defend himself...I was just hiding
it...

ERIC

'Just' hiding it...someone else 'just' pulls the
trigger...some kid 'just' gets his head shot off!

RYAN

I didn't think it would happen...Zac asked me
as a favour...to hold it for just one night...

ERIC

Did he pay you?

Silence.

ERIC (CONT'D)

Did he?

RYAN

Brought me to the games...nightclubs...gave
me 200 pounds...after a week I told him I
wanted to get rid of it...but he just laughed
and shook his head...

ERIC

Why doesn't he hold it?

RYAN

Back to prison for years if he gets caught...but
he needs it close...He can get it from me in
five minutes...

ERIC

And if you get caught?

Ryan struggles.

RYAN

I'll do five years Eric...minimum.

ERIC

Fuck! Five years of your life Ryan.

Ryan nearly breaks down.

RYAN

He shot someone...

ERIC

A drug dealer?

RYAN

No Eric...you have no idea...someone insulted
him at the club...

ERIC

Jesus Christ...Did he kill him?

Ryan hangs his head in shame. Pause.

RYAN

No...in the back...he'll live...I didn't see
it...he told me when he gave me back the gun.

Eric jumps up and grabs the gun.

> ERIC
>
> Right...we're going to the police now! Come on! Right now.

Ryan runs at him and clutches him desperately.

> RYAN
>
> No Eric...please...you can't do that...listen to me...

Eric tries to fight him off as he struggles to get to the door.

> RYAN (CONT'D)
>
> You can't do it!

> ERIC
>
> Why the fuck not! Tell them everything...

Ryan breaks down and starts sobbing.

> RYAN
>
> They said they'd set the dogs on Jess!

Eric stops in shock and turns to him.

> RYAN (CONT'D)
>
> They've done it before...I heard them talking...Please Eric...they'll fucking do it...tear the face off him...rip him apart! Ah Christ...

Eric can't believe his ears. He stops at the door.

> ERIC
>
> I can't believe this...what's going on?

RYAN

If I run off...they'll do Jess. I know they will.

Eric moves back to a seat and collapses.

ERIC

I've got to go and speak to him...

RYAN

They're not like you...not like your
mates...they don't give a fuck.

ERIC

We can't live like this...we can't go to the
police...you can't run off...[Pause] I'm going
to find him...

RYAN

Don't do it...promise me.

ERIC

Give me his number...

RYAN

No! He'll go fucking crazy!

ERIC

Give me it Ryan or that's us finished. I mean
it.

Eric pulls out his phone. Long moment.

RYAN

619543677 [as Eric dials] Oh shit...

Ryan looks sick with nerves as the phone rings out.

Eric shakes his head as the answering machine clicks on.

                              ERIC
                    This is Eric Bishop here…[a look between
                    them] Ryan's dad…[it registers with Ryan].
                    I've got to see you as soon as possible…please
                    phone me back at once…

He turns off the mobile.

                         ERIC (CONT'D)
                    Fuck! We've got to find him…you could get
                    done for attempted murder! Rot the rest of
                    your life behind bars…Has the penny fucking
                    dropped?!

Eric dials another phone number.

                         ERIC (CONT'D)
                    [At speed] Meatballs…do me a favour man…
                    I can't come to work…can't tell you now…
                    something cropped up at Jess's school…Fuck!
                    I know they're on my back! Tell them Jess
                    had an accident…okay…see you later…
                    thanks.

Ryan, with the truth sinking in, stares at Eric as he dials
another number.

                         ERIC (CONT'D)
                    Lily…can you phone me back when you get
                    this?…I can't pick up Daisy…can you do it?
                    Speak later…

He checks his watch.

ERIC (CONT'D)

Shit…she's at work and has the phone
off…[frustration] Fuck!…I'll have to go and
face her! Will that prick phone me back?

RYAN

I don't know…

Eric stares at him for a moment. He looks a sorrowful picture.

40. HEALTH CLINIC – RECEPTION

Eric, with his face even more bruised, waits impatiently in
reception for Lily. She comes out wearing a white uniform.
She is stunned to see his face.

LILY

Oh my God Eric…what happened?

ERIC

Dissatisfied customer…goes with the job…

LILY

That's terrible…have you seen a doctor?

ERIC

Fine…nothing…

LILY

Are you okay for the weekend?…I'll cook if
that eye's too sore…

ERIC

Looks worse than it is…

LILY

But who did it?

ERIC

Some nutter...upset with the world and took it out on me...Listen Lily...

LILY

[Cutting him off] A total stranger?

ERIC

He just opened the door...whack! Listen Lily...can I ask you a big favour? I can't pick up Daisy...been some hassle at school with Jess and I've got to sort it out...

LILY

I can't...it's Friday...got appointments all afternoon...

ERIC

Ah shit...I'll have to phone Sam...

LILY

No! She's got an exam today...get her all nervous...can you not ask the school to wait till Monday?

ERIC

Really serious...the headmaster's going crazy and wants to see us...

LILY

About what?

ERIC

He's been accused of bullying...but it wasn't him...I know it wasn't...I just can't let him down...he's really upset...

Lily stares at him for a long moment.

> LILY
>
> Okay…I'll try and get someone to cover me…

> ERIC
>
> Thanks Lily…I'm really sorry…

> LILY
>
> You are telling me the truth Eric? It's not
> something else?

> ERIC
>
> Of course I am…

> LILY
>
> After all we've been through…I need to know
> we are frank with each other…I mean that.

Long moment.

> ERIC
>
> Me too…I feel the same.

She looks at him for a long moment.

> LILY
>
> Okay.

41. STREET OUTSIDE SECURITY OFFICE

Eric's car pulls up outside the office.

Fenner, Zac's sidekick, out on the street, bangs on the office window.

Zac and three others [including Busby his other close mate] exit the office.

Winston, his pit bull, trots out after them.

Zac talks to his mates for a few moments as he glances over at Eric.

Zac and Fenner move towards Eric's car.

Fenner begins to film Eric with a little DVD recorder which makes him very uncomfortable.

Without waiting to be asked Zac jumps into the passenger seat.

> ZAC
>
> [Staring at him] How are you Jack?

> ERIC
>
> Fine thanks...name's Eric.

> ZAC
>
> Jack Nicholson...Cuckoo's nest...[chuckling]
> ...in with the loonies and padded jackets...
> malicious rumours we heard about you...best
> to ignore them...

Fenner, still with the camera, moves closer, and jokes with the others by the office door who are still playing with the dog.

> ERIC
>
> Why is he filming? Please ask him to stop it.

> ZAC
>
> Creative type...needs to express himself...

Zac is smiling at the man outside.

> ERIC
>
> I don't want any trouble...for me or the
> boys...that's why I had to see you face to
> face...

ZAC

Much appreciated...no monkey business eh?

ERIC

Thanks...You've got to take this back...I'll
keep my mouth shut...

He tries to hand over the gun which half reveals itself under
the cloth.

ZAC

'Got to?' [Chuckling] Can't touch that...more
germs than a sailor's dick!

ERIC

Please...leave us alone...

ZAC

I can't have a little cunt like Ryan telling me
what to do...Know my nickname? [Pause] The
Prophet...can sense the future...you're going
to waddle back home...tail between your
legs...unroll the carpet...up with the
floorboard...and pop it back in...

Eric shakes his head.

ZAC (CONT'D)

Oh yes you are...

ERIC

I can't...if you don't take it...I'll throw it
away...

ZAC

Let's just reflect on that for a few minutes...
and let me know...

ERIC

I won't change my mind…

ZAC

I respect that…

He waves over at his boys by the door.

ZAC (CONT'D)

James Stewart…man of principle…

As Zac jumps out Busby and another march across. Busby now has the dog as Fenner continues to film.

Suddenly one pulls a hammer from behind his back and smashes the window beside Eric's head.

Busby hurls Winston the pit bull through the window, but still hangs onto his studded collar.

Eric scrambles in desperation to the passenger seat as the dog pulls wildly against the collar to rip at Eric.

Zac at the other side holds the passenger seat closed as Eric scrambles desperately to escape.

BUSBY

[Sending dog into a fury] Go on Winston! Go my son…Fetch his nose! [Singing] How much is that doggy in the window…the one with the waggly tail…how much is that doggy in the window…I do hope that doggy's for sale…

All the men are laughing, as Fenner continues to film the show.

Eric strains in terror as the pit bull's yellow teeth snap at him from inches away.

It leaps again and grabs the thick padding to Eric's jacket and twists it in a fury as he tries to get more purchase on the grip.

Eric screams as the dog howls ferociously.

> ERIC
>
> OK…I'll do it!

> ZAC
>
> Can't hear you!

Eric screams in desperation.

> ZAC (CONT'D)
>
> Sitting on the fence eh?

The men laugh louder as the dog fights harder and harder to get at him as Busby hangs on desperately. The dog is inches from Eric's body.

FROM ZAC'S POV: He stares down at Eric's terrified face pounding at the passenger window.

> ZAC (CONT'D)
>
> Want to sleep on it?

Zac relinquishes. He lets go of the door and Eric collapses on to the pavement at his feet as the camera man moves closer.

Eric sobs.

> ERIC
>
> I'll do it!…I'll do what you want! Anything…I beg you! Leave me alone.

> ZAC
>
> Very good Jack…real tears…a fucking Oscar contender that. [Pause, whisper in his ear]

How do you think Jess would cope? Eh? Does
he like pets?

The men chuckle even more. Zac turns to Fenner still with the
camera.

                    ZAC (CONT'D)
    Cut!

They piss themselves as they head for the office.

                    ZAC (CONT'D)
        'How much is that doggy...' [high fiving]
        Fucking classic man!

Eric, humiliated, clambers from his knees.

42. ROAD AND ROUNDABOUT

Eric, traumatised, drives home.

He can feel a sense of panic overwhelm him as he approaches a
roundabout.

He's on it now, and can feel the road rush at him. He begins to
circle. He goes round it once, and again.

                    ERIC
        [Shouting] Help me Eric!!

He clutches at the steering wheel, forces himself off, and shoots
towards an exit.

43. ERIC'S HOUSE

Eric wanders into the house.

The boys hear his steps and come out into the hall.

What did he say?

Eric ignores them and plods up the stairs and then enters Ryan's room.

They follow him up.

From the door they watch Eric unroll the carpet, unpick the floorboard. He glances up at them. He then slips the gun back into place.

He replaces everything and then sits back on Ryan's bed. He is pale and trembling.

ERIC

I tried boys...

First Jess sits on the bed beside him. Ryan stares at him. He notices his trembling hands, his dirty clothes, and the lumps torn out of his jacket.

Ryan slowly moves to the bed and sits on the other side beside Eric too. He lays his hand on Eric's arm.

44. ERIC'S HOUSE

In the street outside, Lily and Sam pushing Daisy in a pram walk along towards Eric's home.

SAM

This is weird...isn't it?

Lily just smiles.

SAM (CONT'D)

Are you nervous?

LILY

Don't know…memory plays tricks…it really
confuses me when I see Daisy in his arms…
reminds me of you.

It touches Sam.

SITTING ROOM:

Eric, Ryan, Sam, Lily and Daisy sit round the table after a
meal.

Eric is having great fun with Daisy who makes a total mess
with a yogurt, splattering her hands in the gooey mess. Eric
tries to turn a spoonful into a special delivery from outer space,
but when it arrives in her mouth it is promptly spat out.

Sam notices Lily watching Eric, who is unaware of the eyes
upon him. A moment between mother and daughter as they
watch Eric with Daisy.

Jess appears with a crispy apple crumble which impresses all.

LILY (CONT'D)

Did you make that? I don't believe it…

JESS

Off the net…

ERIC

Had to bribe him…would have been cheaper
to buy it from a five star restaurant.

Sam pours more wine into their glasses.

SAM

[Holding up her drink] Here's to you both…I
nearly gave up…I could never have managed
without you…

161

LILY

Don't tempt fate!

SAM

My supervisor said my dissertation was 'first class'! I'm a bit late but he thinks they'll approve it in time so I can graduate with the others.

Eric smiles. He's amazed and delighted for her.

ERIC

You deserve it darling...

SAM

I just needed a good run at it...time instead of a scrambled panic...it's given me so much confidence.

She glances from one to the other.

SAM (CONT'D)

Honestly...thank you...

They chink glasses.

ERIC

I'm really proud of you...

LILY

Me too...

Eric and Lily catch each others's eye as they sip.

JESS

What are you doing?

SAM

Teacher training...primary...

Won't get much for that.

Sam and Lily smile politely but Lily catches Eric's face and can see his disappointment.

Eric gathers up some dirty dishes and takes them into the kitchen.

KITCHEN:

He lays the dishes in the sink. He seems overcome and holds his head in his hands as he leans on the counter.

Unknown to him, Lily enters behind him with more dirty dishes.

She watches him for a moment.

LILY

Are you okay Eric?

ERIC

I'm fine…just a headache I can't get rid of…

LILY

Hope it isn't us…

She moves closer to him – something about his eyes – he's obviously upset by something.

ERIC

No…it's been a lovely night…honestly…

LILY

What is it then?

He hesitates.

ERIC

It's the boys...it's a long story...I've just got to
figure out how to cope.

LILY

There's something's wrong...what is it?

Eric looks like he's trying to find a way to say something, but
then cuts it off.

ERIC

Shit...no point moaning...just need some time
to figure it all out...

Lily looks at him, thinking.

LILY

Sometimes you have to risk it...share things?

She gives him another opportunity to speak his mind. He
wavers, and then shuts down again.

ERIC

I'll get there...fancy a coffee?

Suddenly there is a thunderous crash as the front door is
smashed down. Terrified shouts from the boys above and
pounding feet. They hear Sam scream which sets off Daisy too.

VOICES

[Shouting] Police! Police! Police! Nobody
move!

[Six armed police with body armour stream in. Each officer
has a Glock handgun in a holster and carries a Heckler Kosh
sub-machine gun in his hands. Two crash into the room where
the boys, Sam and baby are, two sprint up stairs and two rush
into the kitchen where Eric and Lily are. Each officer is

164

connected up to a radio mike so that they are in contact with 'containment officers' outside the house. As soon as armed officers realise there is a young mother and baby in the house – something that they would not have realised until that moment – they will radio for a policewoman from the containment contingent outside to come in as quickly as possible as soon as they judge it is safe to do so. It all happens in a flash.]

FROM ERIC AND LILY'S POV: They see two armed officers rush towards them.

> OFFICER 1
>
> On the floor! Now!

> LILY
>
> Oh my God! My daughter has her baby!

> OFFICER 1
>
> On the floor!!

> ERIC
>
> What the hell do you want?

Officer 2 points his machine gun and screams at Eric.

> OFFICER 2
>
> Shut up! On the floor. Now!!

Lily is beside herself as she hears Sam and the baby crying from the other room.

Officer 2 forces Lily and Eric to the floor in the kitchen.

> OFFICER 2 (CONT'D)
>
> Hands behind your back! Now!

Officer 2 then handcuffs them with plastic cuffs. [Once they are secure Officer 1 disappears to help search upstairs.]

Eric and Lily, both stunned, lie side by side. They can hear the commotion from the other room.

LILY
That's my granddaughter! Please let me go to her...

OFFICER 2
A female police officer is dealing with her. Do what you are told Madam...and we'll get the baby and mother out of here as soon as possible...

Officer 2 quickly frisks Eric on the ground [from head to toe] but doesn't touch Lily.

ERIC
What's this all about?

POLICEMAN
Quiet Sir and do what you are told. We have a warrant to search this house for a firearm...

Eric looks across at a traumatised Lily whose face is on the ground close to him.

LILY
I can't believe this...

Lily and Eric hear Sam scream from the other room.

SAM
Put those bloody guns away! My baby's terrified!

POLICEWOMAN
Please calm down Madam and we'll have you out of here as soon as possible...

SAM

Where's my mother? We're not criminals…I
want to go home with my baby…

Eric is shamed as Lily's eyes fill with tears.

Officer 2 moves to the kitchen door so that he has a view of
the corridor to front entrance and of Eric and Lily lying on
the kitchen floor. As he reports to the containment officers
outside via radio [along lines of male and female secured and
cuffed but need of a policewoman to search the female] Lily
has a chance to whisper to Eric who lies beside him.

LILY

[Whispered] What the hell is going on Eric?

ERIC

I don't know…

LILY

[Quietly furious] Stop lying to yourself! They
are looking for a gun! Are the boys in a gang?

Eric can't reply.

LILY (CONT'D)

[Whispering furiously] Look at me…[at last he
makes eye contact]…is there a gun in your
house?

Eric shakes his head as he confronts a fearsome Lily.

LILY (CONT'D)

If you asked me…my daughter…my
granddaughter into your house with a gun in
it…know what that means Eric? Eh?

ERIC

Yeah...I know what that means Lily...

LILY

What really happened to your eye?

He can't look at her.

LILY (CONT'D)

Eric...What happened?

He can't answer.

A policewoman comes into the kitchen and helps Lily to her feet.

POLICEWOMAN

Can you come this way please Madam?

LILY

What do you want with me?

POLICEWOMAN

I have to search you Madam. After that you
will all have to come down to the station to
give a statement...

Lily shakes her head in resignation. As she leaves she catches sight of Eric's despondent face stare up at her pathetically from the floor.

ERIC

[To himself] Ah Jesus...

44B. OUTSIDE ERIC'S HOUSE

Eric, Ryan and Jess are led to a waiting police van and put inside.

Sam, Daisy and Lily are led to a police car by the same policewoman.

Both car and van head off towards a police station.

ERIC'S HOME:

Four plain clothes CID officers pull the house apart, systematically.

Miscellaneous: officers search behind shelves, under furniture. Every box and cupboard is examined.

Kitchen: every pot and container has been emptied. One officer examines inside the fridge. He empties the contents, including a jumbo chicken, on to the table.

> CID OFFICER 1
>
> [To another] Nothing here...

Ryan's bedroom: CID officers 3 and 4 are pulling out drawers, rifling through cupboards. They roll up the carpet and spot the loose floorboards. One man investigates.

> CID OFFICER 3
>
> Something here...

He fishes out a plastic bag and gives it to his colleague. He examines it.

> CID OFFICER 4
>
> Not much...

He tosses it on the bed. Officer 3 feels again under the floorboards for as long as his arm will reach.

> CID OFFICER 3
>
> Nothing...

Another officer enters.

> CID OFFICER 1
>
> That's it…wrap it up.

> CID OFFICER 3
>
> What a cock-up…a baby and no gun…

> CID OFFICER 4
>
> …they got an emergency call from a reliable
> source…a life in danger and loaded gun…
> damned if you do…damned if you don't…

> OFFICER 1
>
> Somebody's head is going to roll…

ERIC'S HOME – EVENING:

A police van pulls up and drops off Eric, Ryan and Jess.

They move towards their house and pass by a fresh-faced young police constable who has been guarding the front door.

> CONSTABLE
>
> You might need to get the door fixed. Good
> night.

The constable heads off as Eric and boys enter their home.

Ryan sprints up the stairs to his room.

Eric walks through to the kitchen and confronts the chaos.

Jess follows. They stare around at the ransacked kitchen. They hear Ryan sprint down the stairs and he rushes into the kitchen.

RYAN

I don't get it...they've lifted the floorboard...
where the hell is it?

Eric pulls the chicken towards him, cracks it open a bit — rams
his hand up its innards — and delivers the gun wrapped in
plastic, which he drops on the table with a thud.

RYAN (CONT'D)

I can't believe it...

ERIC

Nor could the chicken.

RYAN

[Hesitant] What did Lily say?

Eric stares at him.

Ryan looks mortified.

Ryan's phone rings. He recognises the number. Panic on his
face.

RYAN (CONT'D)

It's him...Zac.

ERIC

Put it on speaker...Do it.

He does so and answers.

RYAN

It's me...

ZAC

Are they gone?

                    RYAN
        Fuck…how did you know?

Zac just laughs.

                    ZAC
        Still got the heat Ryan…eh? [Pause] Don't
        want to upset Winston…do we?

                    RYAN
        Still got it…

                    ZAC
        Good…knew you had brains…Think this calls
        for a fat bonus eh? Did you hear me?

                    RYAN
        Heard you.

                    ZAC
        I'll need it soon. Very soon.

The phone goes dead.

                    ERIC
        So what are you going to do Ryan? Let that
        fucker shoot some kid in the back for calling
        him names and then stick it under your bed
        again?

Ryan looks shamed.

                ERIC (CONT'D)
        Running around in a fancy car like a spruced
        up little prick messing up other people's lives!
        Your brother's! Sam's…Lily's…

                            JESS

And yours Eric.

                            ERIC

[Almost resigned] Yeah...mine. Don't give a
fuck about anyone but yourself...selfish little
shit...I'm ashamed of you! Ashamed of me! If
we ever get through this...things are going to
change round here.

They all look at each other and the gun between them. Ryan's
mobile buzzes with a text. He checks it.

                            RYAN

Ah fuck...from Zac...better see this.

SITTING ROOM:

Eric, Jess, and Ryan stare at the computer screen.

Eric watches images of himself inside his car screaming in
terror as the pit bull snaps at his shoulder.

We hear laughter from the men and commentary from Zac,
but the latter's face has been blanked out digitally.

There is a horrible shot of Eric's face all contorted as he presses
against the passenger window. More laughter as the men watch.
The video zooms in on the snot, tears and Eric's traumatised
face.

Jess begins to break.

                            JESS

Stop it! I can't stand it!

                            ERIC

Leave it.

At last Zac lets Eric out of the car. He tumbles to the ground, sobbing desperately, and pleads for mercy on his knees.

> ZAC'S VOICE
>
> Cut!

Men's laughter.

Eric stares at the screen which has turned to black and confronts his own reflection.

Ryan and Jess, both stunned, stare at Eric with deep concern.

> RYAN
>
> I'm so sorry Eric…

45. ERIC'S ROOM – NIGHT

Eric, with what remains of the wine before him, is highly agitated as he confronts Cantona.

> ERIC
>
> …can't fucking cope…humiliated…How
> many are watching this? Sniggering their
> fucking heads off as I crawl on the pavement…
> [deep confusion] nearly ripped my face off!
> Like a horror movie…passed around like a
> sick joke…Do they know I'm real man…or
> they just don't give a fuck? [Long pause] What
> can I do?

Silence as he stares at Cantona for a few moments.

> CANTONA
>
> Always more choices than you think…
> always…

Another fucking shave?!

Long pause.

CANTONA

Your teammates.

ERIC

Can't tell them...my boy holding a gun for a
jerk who shoots kids in the back! I'm too
ashamed...what will they think?

CANTONA

Trust them...

46. BAR

Eric, Jack, Spleen, Monk, and Ryan sit round a table in the
corner of the pub.

They all stare at their drinks in total silence as they think.
There is the occasional sigh and shake of the head as they
contemplate.

Eric is opposite Spleen [who is wearing a FC United top].

The door crashes open and Meatballs strides in.

He squeezes in beside them, and then pulls out a brand new
book.

MEATBALLS

Psychopaths!

They all stare in amazement at the book [same title] as he slaps
it down on the table.

MEATBALLS (CONT'D)

They don't give a flying fuck!

MONK

Is that the most recent research from Stanford?

MEATBALLS

No negotiation…no reasoning…the only thing
you can do…is frighten the shit out of them!
Make them realise it's not just worth it.

JACK

Gang of thugs…muscles coming out their ears!
Dogs! Guns! Baseball Bats! What the fuck have
we got?

SPLEEN

No violence…or we're sunk…can't compete
with that…

JACK

We've been through every option…there's
nothing we can do. Take your chance with the
police…

MONK

Means you'll have to move…go and hide…

MEATBALLS

He can't do that…he'll need us close…

Silence again. Eric notices the empty glasses.

ERIC

Same again…

Eric moves up to the bar and orders the drinks.

25

26

27

28

29

30

32

31

33

34

35

36

37

38

39

40

41

42

43

45

44

46

47

48

49

50

51

52

53

54

CANTONA

'He that sews thistles...shall reap prickles.'

An incredulous Eric turns to see Cantona by his side pouring from a bottle of champagne into a delicate glass with long stem.

CANTONA (CONT'D)

If they are faster than you...don't try and outrun them. [Pause] If they are taller...don't out jump them...if they are stronger on the left...you go right. [Pause, smile] But not always...[Pause] Remember...to surprise them...got to surprise yourself first...

The pints arrive. Eric looks to his side, but Cantona is gone. Eric lays down the pints.

More silence as they all take a solemn sip.

ERIC

What's he frightened of?

They look at him, thinking.

JACK

Other gangs? Police? His granny...who knows?

MONK

Beat them black and blue...come up smiling to spite you...

MEATBALLS

Hard as nails...scared of nothing...

Eric shakes his head.

ERIC

...of losing face.

Silence. They are all impressed as they consider the possibility.

MONK

If we could only take the piss...embarrass
him...

JACK

Something...unexpected...so the fucker leaves
you alone...

MONK

Yeah...that would be the ticket.

JACK

Easier said than done...

Pause.

RYAN

YouTube.

Silence. They all turn to stare at him. Eric's eyes light up.

MEATBALLS

What the fuck's that...a new brylcreem?

ERIC

That's it.

Eric looks at Spleen.

ERIC (CONT'D)

When's the next home game?

Eric looks up over the shoulders of his mates towards the bar.
From the distance Cantona toasts Eric with his long-stemmed

glass of champagne, winks at him, and then knocks back the drink in one.

47. STREET OUTSIDE ZAC'S HOUSE

Meatballs, Eric and Jess walk along the street towards Zac's house.

Meatballs carries a big long pole with noose at the end of it.

Jess carries a dainty little digital recorder.

> MEATBALLS
> Have you enough film in that contraption?

Jess shakes his head and just laughs.

> JESS
> You worry about the dog…it's a killer.

> MEATBALLS
> I'm a postman…could write a book about the bastards.

They get to a corner. They peer at the house and wait. Eric checks his watch.

> MEATBALLS (CONT'D)
> Have you got the sausages?

Eric nods.

48. DUAL CARRIAGEWAY – SUPPORTERS' BUS

> SPLEEN
> Bus number one…are you receiving me?

Spleen is standing at the front of a bus full of FC United fans. He is on his mobile, and is dressed in half khaki like a marine in action.

Fans in the front seat are pissing themselves.

FAN 1

It's another bus Spleen…not outer space!

SPLEEN

[Ignoring them] Bus number two…are you
receiving me? Bus number three…Bus number
four…Bus number four…Where the fuck are
you?

FAN 2

You've got to say 'Roger…over and out!'

SPLEEN

Are you receiving me number four?!

FAN 2

'Over and out' for Christ's sake…

Another bus, marked number four on the window, pulls up
alongside them in a parallel lane. There is another fan at the
front of that bus, just like Spleen in khakis, shouting
instructions into a mobile and getting red-faced too. They are a
mere seven metres apart but don't see each other.

SPLEEN

Bus number four…What is your current
position?

The two fans in the front seat are pissing themselves as they
look across at the other bus.

FAN 1

Like the fucking Yanks in Baghdad! [To
Spleen] There he is there you prick! Three feet
away!

Spleen gives them an angry wave as the bus accelerates past.

> SPLEEN
>
> [Addressing the bus] Right boys…are you
> ready? Operation Cantona!!

> FANS

Yeah!

> SPLEEN
>
> We've got to get this all wrapped up in forty-
> five mins or we'll miss kick off…Right…you
> know the plan…get your Erics out now! And
> let's go for it.

As one they pull out their rubber Cantona masks from their
rucksacks, and slip them on.

> FANS
>
> What a friend we have in Jesus…

BUS 2: Full of supporters pulling on masks.

> FANS (CONT'D)
>
> He's our Saviour from afar…

BUS 3:

> FANS (CONT'D)
>
> What a friend we have in Jesus…

BUS 4:

> FANS (CONT'D)
>
> And his name is Cantona…

Snippets of the chorus and Marseillaise as they slip into smaller
and quieter streets.

49. STREET OUTSIDE ZAC'S HOUSE

Eric, Meatballs, and Jess pull on their Erics as they see the first bus arrive.

First one bus, then another, then another, and then the fourth surround the house on two sides and pull to a halt.

The buses cut their engines. Total suburban silence for a moment.

Loud burst of air breaks.

Jess records the fans, in silence, stream from all four busses.

A dozen men at each bus move to the undercarriage, and extract sledgehammers, crowbars, shovels, picks, trimmers, hedge-cutters and other miscellaneous garden tools.

They are into line again — some 250 Erics.

BY THE GATE:

Meatballs dangles a long string of sausages through the high gate.

> MEATBALLS
> Here Winston...here boy...get your ugly chops
> round that you fucker!

The dog is alert and makes a bee-line for the meat. Meatballs expertly wheeches the noose round the beast's neck and pulls tight.

> MEATBALLS (CONT'D)
> ...off to the vet to get you sorted...

The beast starts howling pitifully as Eric gives the thumbs up to the gang. Meatballs hands the pole to one of the others and then moves to the intercom. He holds up his finger to his mouth to make sure they are all hushed and then presses the buzzer.

VOICE

Who is it?

MEATBALLS

Postman…special delivery.

The electric gate begins to slide open.

[An Eric skips through the gate and grabs the pole attached to the beast from inside the garden now and takes a firm hold.]

MEATBALLS (CONT'D)

[As gang stream through] A little gardening boys…express yourselves…

The hoards stream through. Several start digging up the lawn while others set about the flowers and bushes.

First Zac, then maybe a few girls appear at an upstairs window. Stunned faces and curses as Zac sees a favourite shrub being swung around an Eric's head and then go flying. More bushes are given a severe haircut.

Zac bursts from the front door in his Y-fronts holding a baseball bat and stares at the unbelievable sight in front of him. His mates Fenner and Busby join him.

ZAC

What the fuck do you think you're doing? [He gives a loud piercing whistle] Winston!

The dog yelps pathetically. He catches sight of the beast attached to the pole.

ZAC (CONT'D)

What the fuck are they wearing?

BUSBY

Jesus…looks like Cantona…by the dozen.

They stare in amazement as dozens of Erics – chanting 'Red Army' – now attack his Greek statues – bang, the leg of one goes flying – while at another spot several start to demolish his greenhouse.

FENNER

Fucking hooligans!

Zac can't believe his eyes as a pair of Erics jump up on to the roof of his car and start dancing to the above chant. Several others join them on the boot. 'Red Army!!'

ZAC

Get off my fucking car!

Two girls run out to see what's happening. They shriek at the mayhem. The head of another statue pops off and rolls along.

Several others pull at the third statue with a rope. It collapses like Saddam Hussein, with an extended arm.

A group of three Erics piss up against the wall as Zac fumes.

BUSBY

Bastards…what can we do?

FENNER

There's too many…

ZAC

Fuck you!

Zac charges towards those dancing on his car, but is stopped dead as he is struck by two paint bombs covering his Y-fronts in red paint.

FANS

Charge!!

Some three dozen charge them with paint guns and water pistols. Zac, Fenner, Busby and girls run inside as it is all filmed by Jess.

Several men move up with sledgehammers and smash it down.

Dozens of fans charge into the house and corner Zac and co in the huge sitting room. Paint bombs splatter the entire room. Walls, sofas, ceilings are blasted in a sea of colour.

Zac is furious, but terrified by the numbers. They are totally plastered in paint and soaked by dozens of water pistols but are too frightened to do anything about it as they confront several men with crowbars.

ZAC

Very very very fucking funny...what do you bastards want?

He spots an Eric [Jess] filming him with a recorder.

ZAC (CONT'D)

Turn that fucking thing off!

He backs off as an Eric lifts a crowbar.

JESS

[Filming]...You're going to look great in front of your fans...

ZAC

[Screaming] Turn it off!

He makes a move towards the camera but backs off as two fans with crowbars step in beside Jess.

                         JESS
            Would you like to say hello to anyone?

Several of the fans are pissing themselves, while others continue to blast the walls with the paint guns.

                         ZAC
            What the fuck do you want?

A huge figure makes his way to the front.

Silence. He then throws a gun on the ground before Zac. [Delicate floor tiles.]

                      MEATBALLS
            Recognise this?

Zac shakes his head.

Meatballs moves over to a luxury-sized monster-slim-fit TV. He clicks it gently with the sledgehammer, and the screen shatters.

                   MEATBALLS (CONT'D)
            Clumsy me…

He moves over to a glass dining table and smashes the hell out of that too.

                   MEATBALLS (CONT'D)
            Do you recognise it now?

                         ZAC
            OK…what do you want?

                      MEATBALLS
            Now for my next trick…right in front of your

eyes Ladies and Gentlemen…I'm going to
smash this little fucker into pieces!

Meatballs takes an almighty swing with the hammer…smash!!

He misses by a mile as it disintegrates the tiles. The gun
bounces. He swings and misses again. More smashed tiles.

MEATBALLS (CONT'D)
Fuck!

Fans are in knots as Zac and his mate stare in terror.

He swings again. Misses. More destruction.

More laughter.

MEATBALLS (CONT'D)
Fucking hell! It keeps moving on me…

Another fan takes over. Bingo. It smashes the gun. The barrel is
badly dented and bent.

FAN 1
Can shoot round corners with that…

MEATBALLS
You know where that came from?

Zac nods.

MEATBALLS (CONT'D)
If you go near that family again…know what
we'll do? [Silence] Come on you wanker!
Thought you could tell the future?! We'll come
back with ten fucking bus loads…and we'll
demolish your whole fucking house brick by
brick by brick…One word with Ryan
[pointing at camera] and this is on the Tube…

187

JESS

YouTube for fuck's sake…

MEATBALLS

Whatever the fuck it is…you'll be on it…in
there in your see-through Y-fronts you fucking
poncy twat and everybody laughing at your
tiny red dick…Fancy that? I asked you a
question asshole.

Zac shakes his head.

MEATBALLS (CONT'D)

And if you run…hide…sneak off to a fucking
rabbit hole in the outer Hebrides we'll find
you…know why? [Pause, as Jess moves closer
with recorder] Because I'm a fucking postman!

The other fans really enjoy this.

JESS

[With the camera] Can you say that again…
that was very good…

MEATBALLS

Don't mess with Her Majesty's fucking Royal
Post Office you useless wank!

As the fans piss themselves Zac and Fenner, soaking wet,
holding their bollocks, look at the ground, while Meatballs,
chest stuck out, head held high, struts round the room, like
Cantona of old.

MEATBALLS (CONT'D)
Ooh! Ah! Cantona!…Ooh! Ah! Cantona!

THE REST
Ooh Ah Cantona…Ooh Ah Cantona!

MEATBALLS
[To Zac] Join in you prat…or I'll do your
toilet!

ZAC
[Reluctantly] Ooh Ah Cantona…

Jess moves in closer with the recorder to get a fine close up of
Zac mouthing the chant in among the chaos of his newly
redecorated Pollock-like sitting room.

50. BY A BUS OUTSIDE ZAC'S HOUSE

As the last of the fans stream back onto the bus [some with and
some without their Erics on] an exuberant Meatballs
approaches Eric.

MEATBALLS
Best day since we won the Cup in '99! Did
you see his face? Shitting himself!

ERIC
[Grabbing his arm] Thanks man…you have no
idea…

They glance round at Ryan and Jess who stand by the bus as a
few more fans climb on. Their eyes shine as they examine the
recording they have just taken.

JESS
Eric! Got to see this…we've nailed the bastard!

Eric moves closer between them. The boys laugh as they see a
humiliated Zac chant 'Ooh Ah Cantona' in his Y-fronts among
the dozens of Erics.

JESS (CONT'D)
Won't bother us now…looks such a twat.

Jess and Ryan clap each other's hand. Eric puts his arms around their shoulders as they continue to watch another few moments in triumph.

MEATBALLS
Come on guys move it…we'll miss the game!

A brief moment between Eric and an emotional Ryan.

RYAN
Thanks Eric.

Eric pulls him closer with the arm still around his shoulder. Jess folds back the screen of the recorder.

RYAN (CONT'D)
Have you spoken to Lily?

Eric shakes his head.

ERIC
Won't return my calls…

RYAN
You've got to tell her Eric…she'll understand…

ERIC
It's over…she's had enough…and I don't blame her.

Ryan and Jess glance at each other.

RYAN
Eric…

ERIC

None of your business! Leave it.

MEATBALLS

Come on you pair!

Reluctantly Jess and Ryan clamber on.

Just as the bus is about to move off a single straggling Eric with mask on runs towards the bus. The driver impatiently opens the door.

DRIVER

Fuck's sake Cantona! Move your arse!

Just before he jumps on, the man turns to face Eric, lifts his mask for a brief second and smiles at him. It is Cantona. He enters in a flash, the door closes, and the bus pulls off.

The buses stream past Eric.

He can still hear them singing [perhaps to tune of 'Sloop John B'] above the sound of the engines.

Cantona is now at the back window watching him…he gives Eric a simple wave goodbye.

Eric does the same and watches him grow fainter and fainter.

51. HEALTH CLINIC

Jess and Ryan walk into the clinic.

They are nervous as they peer inside. They spot Lily in the reception bend to talk to someone in a wheelchair.

Jess and Ryan stare at each other, hesitating.

JESS

Fuck…she might go crazy…

RYAN

Come on…we owe him.

They dart in and hang around sheepishly as Lily finishes off talking to the patient.

She catches sight of the boys and stops dead. The boys hang their heads in embarrassment as she approaches.

At last Ryan looks up and starts to speak to her. She listens intently as they tell her the story.

52. OUTSIDE GRADUATION HALL, COLLEGE

A happy group dressed in their best suits and fancy dresses. [Sam, in graduation cloak, Eric, Lily, Daisy, Jess, Ryan, Meatballs, Monk, Jack and Spleen.]

Meatballs, in charge as ever, snaps photographs of them all with Sam in the middle holding her degree scroll.

Daisy, dressed in a beautiful dress, is passed from hand to hand, as they all take a turn with her.

MEATBALLS

Right…enough of you lot…just Sam!

They all step back to leave her alone.

SAM

[Laughing] This is so so embarrassing!!

MEATBALLS

[Peering through camera] Gorgeous sweetheart…[crossing her legs]…just like your father…a postman's legs…

SAM

Meatballs…I'm going to skin you!

Eric, holding Daisy, tentatively stands by Lily. There is a tenderness, but still a wariness between them. They are touched as they watch Sam being photographed, first by herself and then with Jess and Ryan.

ERIC

She looks beautiful...doesn't she?

Lily nods.

LILY

I'm so happy for her...she worked her socks off...she's wanted to be a teacher since she was seven years old.

ERIC

You've done a great job Lily. [Pause] Thanks for calling last night...made it easier...I was so embarrassed to meet you after all that nonsense.

LILY

I know what happened...[Eric is shocked] ...Everything...the boys came to see me.

Eric glances up at them. They are both watching him with some concern and then they smile at him as he shakes his head in amazement.

LILY (CONT'D)

Don't know what I would have done...but it took courage Eric...I'll give you that. [She glances up at Jess and Ryan] And those boys... despite everything...love you to pieces...Sam too. [Pause] You must have done something right.

She holds his eye for a moment. He's overwhelmed.

                              SAM
                I want one with Mum and Dad…come on!

She grabs the camera from Meatballs.

Eric and Lily, hesitant, and then self-consciously, stand together
for a photo as Sam points the camera. She lets the camera drop
for a second.

                        SAM (CONT'D)
                Where in the name of God…Dad…did you
                dig up those shoes?

Eric, holding out his foot, sheepishly looks down at his pointy
blue suede shoes as the others laugh.

Eric and Lily turn to smile at each other. Lily lets out a quiet
chuckle.

                              LILY
                Think I never noticed you lunatic?

                              ERIC
                Lunatic…Moi?

Eric takes her by the waist.

Flash of the camera.

Freezes on their image.

Fade to black.

…and then white flashes on black.

PRESS CONFERENCE – NEWS FOOTAGE 1995:

There are hundreds of flashing cameras reflected on the young Eric Cantona's nervous face as he takes his seat before hundreds of journalists.

Cantona stares at them, and then takes a sip of water.

CANTONA
When the seagulls follow the trawler it is
because they think sardines will be thrown into
the sea...Thank you.

Cast Notes
Steve Evets
John Henshaw
Stephanie Bishop
Lucy-Jo Hudson
Gerard Kearns
Stefan Gumbs
Justin Moorhouse
Des Sharples
Greg Cook
Mick Ferry
Smug Roberts
Johnny Travis

Steve Evets

Eric Bishop

Steve Evets, 49, describes himself as 'just a jobbing actor', but not many jobbing actors have lived like he has.

'I'm a working-class lad from Salford. I left school without a clue what to do but on the last day some guy came in and showed me a film on the Merchant Navy and I thought, "Why didn't you show us this before? No saluting officers, no uniforms…" So I joined the Merchant Navy.'

Three years later he was kicked out. 'I got up to all sorts of things: I jumped ship twice in Japan, I spent my eighteenth birthday in a Bombay brothel – it was really liberating! I was a bit of a loose cannon in them days. Then I got a job delivering industrial pipes for some firm, because I didn't have any other options. I got married and my marriage didn't work out and that firm laid me off. So I decided to follow what was in my head which was to do some kind of acting or something creative.'

He took a foundation course in drama at a local college. 'It was boring, all sort of academically inclined. So I packed that in and I formed my own little street theatre company with two friends.' Extras work, fringe and profit-share theatre all followed. In order to get his Equity card Evets changed his surname from Murphy to the palindromic Evets. He has since dabbled in spoken-word and comedy (performing as Adolph Chip-pan) and music (Evets has played bass with The Fall but has now, as is traditional, fallen out with its lead singer Mark E Smith). But acting is his first love, and latterly there's been television work in everything from *Shameless* to *Heartbeat*.

'It's always been tough going. But I've never been in this thing for the money otherwise I'd have packed it in years ago. I've just stuck to it because you've got to have something you enjoy doing, and this just happens to be what I like.'

For the part of Eric Bishop, a football-mad postman in a tailspin, Ken Loach was looking for native Mancunians, between forty and fifty. Evets went through recall after recall, as part of Loach's usual extensive audition process.

'Ken wants to see what you're made of, how you cope in certain situations, how quickly you think on your feet. He takes his time over the casting because at the end of the day, none of us know what the film is, so we're trusting him. And he's trusting us – because he's spent so much time analysing you.'

Evets got the part without seeing a script or knowing what the film was about. That meant he had no idea that Eric Cantona himself was to be his co-star. 'Shortly after I was cast there was an article in a newspaper and it had a picture of Ken with Cantona at Old Trafford. It said Cantona was co-producing. I didn't for one minute think he'd be in it. When I got the bit of script where my character talks to Eric Cantona the poster, I thought to myself, well, they'll use his voiceover for the poster to talk back at me. At a push I thought that at a certain point where I'm particularly deranged, they might superimpose his face on the poster and have it talk. I never in a million years dreamed that Eric Cantona would be in it to the extent that he is.'

He describes the moment when Loach smuggled Cantona in to the room. 'They'd got him in there like a military operation behind this curtain. There he was, bang, in my room. It was dead surreal. It was like an acid trip condensed into a minute. I was in a scene with Eric Cantona. In the film. And of course when he cut it was like, "My God." Then it was dinner time and they gave me the next bit of script. "This is the scene you're doing with Eric this afternoon. So read it…"'

Evets is not an avid football fan. 'But of course everybody knows about Eric Cantona. He is a legend. Everybody knows about the seagulls thing. Which by the way makes total sense. Anyway, he has kind of adopted Manchester and people love him. I'm still in awe of him, although I have got to know him a bit better. He does seem quite distant, but his distance isn't arrogance. I think he's quite a shy person, a true gentleman.'

In *Looking For Eric*, Evets' character Eric Bishop is a man who has lost his confidence. 'He's one of them guys that has just settled in to a mundane existence. His heart's in the right place. Doesn't always think before he puts his mouth in gear. Couldn't face up to responsibility in the past with his first wife Lily, which is kind of the root of his problems – that and his childhood with a belligerent, bullying father. He's not always been strong enough to say, "No, I'm not having this."'

Enter Cantona. 'He's my mentor in the film. He comes out with these gems of wisdom to help my character build his confidence, get his nerve back and gather a bit of self-respect.'

Evets says Loach encouraged him to ad lib. 'I put in a little bit, yeah. In one scene we're talking about the time he was banned for karate kicking that fan at Palace. I said, "That twat got what he deserved." He didn't seem to mind. And then there was a moment when my character has had it up to here with Cantona's philosophies. I said, "I'm still trying to get my head round the seagulls one for Christ's sake." After that I apologised. He said, "That's okay."'

Evets downplays his talents but people are starting to take notice. Last year he starred in Kenny Glenaan's *Summer*, alongside Robert Carlyle, and *Looking For Eric* is his first lead.

'This whole thing has been a dream job. I hate to pre-empt things by saying this is my break because who knows. I'm a jobbing actor me. Have been for years. This certainly won't do me any harm. But it doesn't matter because I've worked with Ken now, it's an ambition fulfilled. Eric Cantona's in it, I've got the lead role…I mean what actor wouldn't die for that job? It's on my CV and if I never work again, this has been an absolute adventure.'

John Henshaw
Meatballs

John Henshaw is one of several sons of Manchester on the cast of *Looking For Eric* who's been forced to swap shirts.

'I'm a Man City fan. There are a lot of us – it's because we're filming here in Manchester. Most United fans, as you know, live in Essex...'

Henshaw plays Meatballs, the point man of the postmen. 'He's one of the lads at the Post Office. He's a good bloke; he'll stand up for family and friends; he'll stand his corner. He doesn't take any shit and he sees himself as an intellectual. He probably isn't but he's been on more courses than Red Rum. He's a good mate of Eric's, so he's trying to help him out of his current depression. Then the wheels fall off a little bit when Eric's stepson Ryan comes unstuck with a local gangster... Meatballs and the lads are forced to take action.'

Henshaw says he has always wanted to be in a Ken Loach film. 'I worked with Tony Garnett on *The Cops* and he said, "You should work with Ken." I said, "Chance would be a fine thing." Thank God it's happened because I like the way he and his team work.'

Although Henshaw doesn't have scenes with Cantona himself, Loach asked Henshaw to help prepare Cantona for his scenes (in a foreign language) with Steve Evets. Evets, of course, was not told that Cantona himself would be appearing.

'When the cloak and dagger stuff was going on we did a couple of rehearsals myself and Justin [Moorhouse]. We were in on the secret for many days. So next time we saw Steve – to quote him verbatim – he said, 'You bastards! You Loached me!'

Looking For Eric, Henshaw says, is about mates mucking

together. 'It's working-class men making the effort for one of their mates. The primary instinct is, "You kick him, you kick us" – which is great. Without getting preachy, society's broken down now. We don't have the extended family, with aunties and uncles and grandmas and all the rest of it looking after the kids like they did in the old days. Everybody keeps themselves to themselves. It's very rare to see a gang of lads together. I think the last bastions of communal friendship are the workplace and the football – the game. They bring people together, and that's what turns out with this.'

Stephanie Bishop

Lily

The brief for the character of Lily, Eric Bishop's ex-wife, was succinct, but it was ready-made for Stephanie Bishop.

'I read it and thought, "This is just me." It said that she's competent and ordered, she's got a good job in the NHS, she can be guarded at times but there is an enormous amount of warmth there. I thought, "All my life experiences really can slot in to that brief." So I put myself forward for it, got a call from the casting office to say I had a meeting. I will not forget because it was the day before my birthday. It was just a ten-minute chat with Ken. He wanted to know about my life. I got three further recalls from that. They didn't tell me anything about what I might be doing, but I will never forget finally getting the call.'

Bishop is Manchester born and was brought up in Droylsden. Her family moved to Stockport when she was seven and then on to Denton, but she has always been a Mancunian.

'I didn't do a lot at school. I got married when I was twenty-six, but it didn't last that long. At that point I started looking at my life and asking what I was going to do. So I did Extras work for nine or ten years. Best days of my life, I can't tell you. From there I went to a drama teacher called Andy Devine [who plays Shadrach in *Emmerdale*] and stayed with him for just over a year. I had five jobs to pay my mortgage on my own. But once I did my acting class I thought, "I really, really love this." I got a part in a commercial, got an agent, and now this. I've been very, very fortunate.'

In the film, Lily and Eric's relationship fell apart long ago after Eric balked at the responsibilities of fatherhood and settling down. 'They've not seen much of each other really since Eric left her, other than the occasional birthday party for their daughter Sam, so it's never actually come to the point of talking about how it broke down.'

Twenty-odd years have passed, until Sam has a baby herself and Lily and Eric are brought together to look after it. 'That's the point we start trying to build bridges.'

Crucial to Bishop's understanding of their relationship was seeing how her character first fell in love. 'They showed us the filming of the flashback scenes – how we met, at a dance competition, with young actors playing our young characters. It was the best, best thing. You could just see the spark in their eyes. That was vitally important to build on. From the day they met there was that bond there.'

But since Eric left her Lily has moved on. 'I wondered how would this person get over something so bad happening to them? It cuts deep. I think it took a long time to say, "Right, I've got to move on with my life." Now she's got her head screwed on. She retrained to do physiotherapy, she's got a lovely little home, her daughter's moved away so she does really sweet things like go away to the countryside for weekends. So she's at one with herself. But when she's faced with this thing it brings it all flooding back.'

Lucy-Jo Hudson

Sam

Lucy-Jo Hudson suspects that Ken Loach had no idea that she had starred in *Coronation Street* and *Wild At Heart* when he cast her in *Looking For Eric.*

'At the wrap party I was chatting away to Jonathan [Morris, Editor] who's a massive Corrie fan and he went to Ken, "You do realise that she was Killer Katy?" And his face was "What?" Jonathan went, "In *Coronation Street!*" His face was like, "Oh." He didn't have a clue what I'd done before – and thank God, I'm kind of happy about that.'

At twenty-five Hudson is already a TV veteran, but she says that Sam, her character in *Looking For Eric,* is closer to her real self than any part she's played before.

'I'm quite similar to Sam really. I come from a divorced background and I'm a lot older than my years. I think that's what he [Ken Loach] does – chooses you as the character.'

Sam is a twenty-seven year old who has recently had a baby girl. Her parents, Eric and Lily, divorced when she was quite young. 'She became the mediator between her mum and her dad. She's like the parent in all this, trying to tell them what to do, when actually she's the one that needs that guidance from her parents with being a young mum.'

Hudson confesses to not being much of a football fan, so she went to her fiancé Alan Halsall, a diehard Red, for tips. 'There's a few flashbacks in the film where I play a fifteen year old – myself in pig tails with no make-up in a little horrible denim skirt and a Man U top – it was literally me and a load of big sweaty men on a bus chanting Cantona songs. So I had to speak to Alan. "Give me some help, I don't know what I'm singing."'

It wasn't the last time she found herself thrown. 'Halfway through one scene, unexpectedly, there was a big bang on the door. I thought, "Is this part of the scene?" When the police charged in I absolutely shit myself. I was physically shaking. It was great afterwards because me and Steve were going, "We've been Loached! Yay!" All the crew knew; he'd kept it quiet for weeks. But I have to say that should be done on every single job because you don't know what's going to happen next and you get a real reaction. I was crying – and it was real.'

The Stepsons

Gerard Kearns, *Ryan*

'I had no inkling what the film was about when we started filming. You're kept completely in the dark. A bit of script the night before and that's it. The most I thought was that Cantona was producing it. Until Steve Evets told me that he was doing a take and he heard this deep French voice go, "Turn around." And he'd been hiding in the cupboard.

'It was brilliant learning what happens to Ryan. And disappointing at the same time, and then uplifting as well. Ryan's Eric's stepson, a young lad who's finding his way and has got in with the wrong crowd. He's been led down the wrong path, seeing this guy with a car and a big house, suited and booted, taking him to United games. Everything that a young lad admires – and everything that's a shell. Ryan gets led down the path and then ends up in circumstances that he's got no control over.

'I'm a Man City fan. I'm not a bitter Blue but it hurts to have to wear a United shirt – so I wore a blue protesting top underneath.'

Stefan Gumbs, *Jess*

'I'm from Manchester and I'm twenty years old. My background is a bit like Jess's. We're both from Manchester, both like music, we're into video games and girls. Just everything that a teenager is into.

'I told my friends I'd got a part in a film. They wanted to know what I was doing in it. I told them I didn't know yet! It's different but as soon as I got on set I just felt well relaxed because Ken's just a well relaxed guy.

'Jess is from a previous marriage, Eric's his dad and Ryan's his stepbrother. He's a bit of a bad kid. Gets up to mischief and stuff, got friends round the house all the time. My dad's trying to get them out. I don't tidy at all. We don't do anything apart from go out, come back in, sleep, eat, bring friends round, have parties.

'But Jess wants to be loved by his family and he wants his brother and his dad and him to be happy. Behind it all he's a bit of a soft guy.

'One day I was eating my dinner and Cantona just walked past. Me, as a United fan, I was beside myself. So I ran out and phoned my sister. I was just shocked. I couldn't believe I was in a film, then a Ken Loach film, never mind Manchester United. And then Cantona? I've got a picture of him on my mobile now. And I've put it on Facebook.'

The Postmen

Justin Moorhouse, *Spleen*

'I'm a stand-up comedian and a United fan. It was an open casting: they wanted to see comedians. Ken wanted to know what you were about and what your history was. I know Smug and Monk and Mick and Des, so these are my mates in real life as well.

'I play Spleen. So called because he vents his spleen about certain things. He's a postman, a friend of Eric's and he's now an FC United fan. He's quite opinionated about that. What appeals to Spleen about FC United is the democracy of it I think. He does spout some ideology sometimes.'

Des Sharples, *Jack*

'I've been a stand-up for eight years. Before that I worked at a timber yard, bar work, cutting bricks, making garden sheds. All around Manchester.

'I was born in Old Trafford but I'm a City fan. That side of it was quite hard. I play it from the heart as if I am a United fan – but I'm one of them fans who don't sing that much on the coach.

'Jack's my character. He's a workmate and a long-time friend of Eric's – they've been going to football together for years. Jack's more mischievous and a bit slimmer than the others. Bit more of a Jack the Lad.

'I got invited in for a chat with Ken. We were talking about City's glory days, the last of which was '76. Turns out Ken has met Tony Book, City's manager at the time – he played for Bath City, who Ken supports. So we had that in common – we both support unsuccessful teams.'

Greg Cook, *Monk*

'I haven't been a comedian for long – I'm five years in. Before that there's not much in my range of capability I haven't had a bash at – building jobs, pub and club doorman, taxi driver, pubs, been a market trader, worked in the rigs, street sweeper…

'I'm from Blackpool and Ken used to come there watching football back in the day. I'd picked up an old Blackpool player in my cab and that was Jimmy Armfield – Ken remembered him from his playing days, so we talked about that at our first meeting. I kind of surmised there was some sort of football element involved.'

Mick Ferry, *Judge*

'I'm a stand-up comic, a United fan, I live in Oldham, and I started in comedy eleven years ago. Before that I was an upholsterer.

'I play Judge – they call him The Judge because of the hairstyle. It's just my hair, not grown especially for the film I should add. That's how it naturally is. Anyway, The Judge is a bit of a know-all.'

Smug Roberts, *Smug*

'I'm one of the posties. My stage name is Smug too which is good because nobody forgets who I am. I'm a stand-up and I'm also an actor. I did *Buried*, had a small cameo in *24-Hour Party People* and I also did *Phoenix Nights*.

'This is massively different. It's really exciting – sometimes you have bits of script that nobody else has got. It keeps you on your toes.

'We work on the same circuit, the comics. Ken's seen the chemistry between us. Bring a group that have worked together to work together on a film – it's an inspired move in a way.'

Johnny Travis, *Travis*

'I've been a soul singer in Manchester for the last twenty-three years. I was working in Liverpool installing fire cables as a day job, covered in soot, and I got a text from my agent saying, "Johnny, can you act?" I looked at the mess around me and replied, "Yeah, course I can." It had to be better than this. Anyway, I'd seen a few of Ken's films and I just wanted to meet my hero really.

'Travis is one of Eric's friends, a United supporter, as am I. As it's all unfolded it's just been one of the best times of my life. When I found out Eric Cantona was in it I was just buzzing. He's a god in these parts. I asked him what his greatest goal was. He said, "The next one".'

Production Notes
Rebecca O'Brien
Barry Ackroyd
Fergus Clegg
Jonathan Morris
George Fenton
Sarah Ryan

Rebecca O'Brien

Producer

It was Eric who broke the ice. He wanted to do a film about football fans and he brought it to us. Our best territory is France, and like many of the French, he had a wide knowledge of Ken's films. Ken and Paul are known football supporters – there are so many games in their previous work. It was a simple equation.

Pascal Caucheteux, a French producer who has a company called Why Not, and Vincent Maraval, one of the bosses of the sales company Wild Bunch, came over with Eric to discuss Eric's idea. It was a slightly nervous first meeting because Ken was a bit in awe of Eric and Eric was a bit in awe of Ken. Eric had a few ideas that we discussed, then Paul met Eric for a couple of days and chewed the fat. And from that Paul came up with the story of the film.

Because Pascal and Vincent came to us with Eric, they said they would work with us to bring our usual European co-producing partners to the table. It could be a French/British co-production and we could just make it. It's been a really good partnership and it will obviously crystallise with the launch of the film. They brought French money – television money and government support – that we wouldn't normally have because of Eric's involvement and their involvement.

After that I worked with them to get a distributor here. We did one unusual thing, which I've never done before: when the script was ready, Pascal and Vincent came over and we invited all the main distributors in the UK to pitch to us as to why they wanted to have the film. They were all very interested because you just said Cantona and Ken and the combination was just like 'Bing!' We've worked with Icon before so we were very happy to do that again, and then Channel 4 came on board as well.

What was particularly nice about having the cashflow support from the French was that it meant that I could get on with the job of just getting the film made. I'm so used to being bogged down in the legals but the French took a large part of the weight off my shoulders. It was a very liberating experience and I hope to work with them again.

When it came to filming we tried to keep a low profile in Manchester and not let Little Eric, as we called Steve, know that Eric Cantona was arriving. Trying to smuggle Big Eric in and out of Manchester was hilarious. The first time he came over, he came to do some rehearsal and meet some of the people in the film – but not Steve. That was when we got to go to a match at Old Trafford, which was something else. It was the Champions' League Quarter Final vs Roma, the second leg. We went with Eric, and by the time we actually reached the inner sanctum of the directors' box we were on telly, because they had filmed him arriving. Word was out that Eric was in town.

It took us half an hour to get to our seats. Then once we were in Eric went down to see the boys in the changing room and he brought Sir Alex [Ferguson, Manchester United manager] back with him. This is quarter of an hour before the match. Sir Alex comes in and he shakes Ken warmly by the hand, says hello to me and starts talking about *The Wind That Shakes the Barley*. He said he's seen it several times – he started quoting from the film.

At half time they made an announcement over the tannoy that Eric was in the building. It's something else, having 70,000 people singing to the man next to you. He signed autographs for twenty minutes before the match started and then going through to backstage afterwards, as you walked through people were pinned against the wall. It was as if they'd been touched by his presence. It was an extraordinary event, and that was before we started making the film.

This film is certainly different to *It's A Free World*, or *The Wind That Shakes the Barley*, but we always try and make each film as different as we can from the one before. We haven't done a film with a light heart for a long time. This, dare I say it, is a romantic comedy really, and it's quite a while since we've made something like that.

Barry Ackroyd
Director of Photography

Ken and I have done twelve or thirteen films together and Ken is always very much the master of the set. He knows what he wants to get from the actors, the sound and the location – and from the camera. For the first two or three films I worked on with Ken I was just doing what I was told, but saying, 'Yeah, yeah, that's right. The camera should be here, you're quite right Ken…' I think I've worked all that process out now and I try to contribute something. But it's a matter of fulfilling a brief that is very particular to Ken. The key thing you've got to do as a cinematographer is not to occupy the space that belongs to the actors or the performers or the story. You have to know how to light something that will give that space to the actors again.

This film is like magic with social realism. You wouldn't want to step too far outside of the norms and the look of a Ken Loach film. But other times you wanted to add a little something. Sometimes they were almost coincidental: Eric would sit down and we'd have the back of a sofa or a chair behind him, things suggesting to me that they were wings. Like he was kind of an angel.

I've always tried to add something to each film. Originally Ken never moved the camera unless it was a handheld and it was running or chasing or pushing in to something. Now we occasionally might just move the camera – probably off a vehicle or something like that. The truth of the matter is that Ken gets what he wants. We might all be thinking we're working to a separate brief sometimes – I have my agenda, an actor might think they're improvising, saying just what they think they want to say at this point. And actually you find out we're doing pretty much what Ken Loach likes – which is to say a great thing to do because he is a master not just of directing films but of the whole construction of films.

I've got to say that every film we've done has always had a huge element of humour in it, no matter what the subject is. One of the tricks Ken always uses is to juxtapose the two – you always get a funny thing before you're going to get the bailiffs knocking on the door or the police coming in or the enemy attacking you. So in a way I don't feel this is a different kind of film.

The element that was slightly different was Eric Cantona. He has this presence. Paul's script understands that Cantona's strengths are not just his football but his philosophy, so it's got both those elements in there in great numbers. It's beautiful and it's funny.

Cantona's very photogenic, a huge personality and has a history you can't ignore. But he's gentle, and he's a very generous guy as well. The strange thing was, I think he was in awe of Ken Loach and that was a lovely thing to see.

Fergus Clegg

Production Designer

After having worked on ten films with Ken this was the most different. Actually they're all different but this was unexpected – from reading the script through to the last day's shooting I was kind of thinking, is this really happening?

We found Eric's house in Chorlton-cum-Hardy, a fantastically named place on the outskirts of Manchester. It's a very nice area but it had obviously become run down. A lot of multiple occupancy flats.

The tricky thing was how rough to make it because it's a fine line – it's quite a large house so we assumed they'd bought the house as a project when Eric was married and then the wife had left home. So it was a great, unfinished work. The place we found had been inhabited by various tenants who'd left just before we were there and it was in a fairly dilapidated state so we had to reconfigure the kitchen and a few other rooms to make them habitable for us and to work as a space. It's all about making it real with Ken, so you go to lengths that you wouldn't normally do with a conventional film. The layering, the ageing of things – you could turn it into a pastiche of how that kind of person would live but Ken is always clear that he wants it as realistic as possible.

When it came to doing Eric's bedroom we read in the script that it is a bit like a shrine.

For the Man United memorabilia we trawled eBay and we had a lot of help from Andy Walsh at FC United. They all collect like lunatics so they've got collectibles going back to the beginning of time and they know it from the inside out. Andy gave us stuff signed by Eric...that he asked us to get re-signed because it had faded slightly. We had the life-size poster that Little Eric talks to specially made.

Our biggest challenge was the Cantona masks. We thought it couldn't be that difficult, but we went everywhere to get them. That was one outcome of our meeting with Cantona at the Roma match. We asked Eric if he could rummage in his attic for a mask. He made a phone call while we were sitting in the back of the car and his brother came up with one.

When it came to recreating Eric's workplace we had no help whatsoever from the Post Office – they would not play ball, wouldn't even let us use the logo. So Ken and I managed to sneak in to a post office sorting room early one morning and we based it on that, building most of it.

Most memorably we did this strange fantasy moment where we had Eric and Little Eric dancing together. We were in a film studio with the two of them, rock and roll music being played, CDs hanging on nylon so you had a strange optical effect of light flashing. People kept rubbing their eyes because they couldn't believe it: we never thought we'd see the day with Ken Loach in a studio doing a pop video.

Jonathan Morris
Editor

Editing *Looking For Eric* was a bit different to usual because we have a character in the film who disappears from time to time onscreen. He's a figment of someone's imagination but there are no special effects. It's done with very, very, very – write this down – clever editing.

Another difference in this one is that we have a couple of football montages. So we do have archive material and a lot of Eric Cantona's great goals to choose from.

Putting that together was great fun. There are three or four DVDs of Cantona's best goals around and Ken said, 'Come up to Manchester and put together a little sequence of about twenty goals so that Steve Evets can have a look.' Steve's not a huge football fan so Ken wanted him to see the character that he is infatuated with. When I was up there it was before filming and this guy came in and said, 'Do you mind mate? If I sit next to you?' I thought, 'Well alright, he's a cleaner or something.' And he sat next to me for a while and it turned out to be Steve – our leading man, just having a look!

We went back to the cutting room and put together sequences of the best goals and then eventually we showed the film to Eric Cantona himself. Ken did get a text from Eric saying thank you, he enjoyed it…but there were a couple of other goals he wouldn't mind us considering. He never said, 'Put them in,' but he wanted us to have a look at one or two that he thought were better than one or two that were in there.

There was one goal that we had left out because he's wearing the green and yellow Man U top – we thought it would confuse people, the non-football fans. But he suggested it and we did put it in – if that's all Eric would ask for it was the least we could do.

As it happens I'm an Arsenal supporter. When I met Cantona for the first time at the screening he came up to me and said, 'You're the Arsenal supporter aren't you?' Which was wonderful. He probably didn't know that the one thing I had made sure of was that there was no goal scored against Arsenal in the film. There was one on the shortlist, a free kick against Seaman. I used my influence and power to make sure that didn't make it in.

George Fenton

Composer

With Ken I don't get a script, in fact he more or less doesn't let me see the film until he's finished it. Then I see it and literally within a day or so we sit down and try and decide where the music is going to go and what it's going to do. Since music is part of the finishing process the emphasis of the film is evident to you by that point.

It's hard for me to be objective about *Looking For Eric* because it stars Eric Cantona, who is one of my greatest heroes. I just sat there beaming the whole way through because he's very, very charismatic.

I did think about whether I had a responsibility to the audience to tell them, 'This is going to be funny,' or, 'It's going to be okay really,' because the story begins with our Eric in a bad way. Sometimes the music needs to stand away from the film slightly and help you through it, rather than intensifying what you see. The hard thing with this film was to do that on one level but at the same time to be faithful to Eric Bishop the character. I have never scored a film in my life that began in a more minimal way; I was very, very anxious about it. But Ken is very brave. I started with the sound of a stand-up bass because it seemed like it was a kind of little signature for the postman. It began like that and then we just stripped things away until we ended up with literally just the bass. Which for a musician is not a happy place to be I can tell you!

When Cantona plays the trumpet, even though he's not a trumpet player there is a magnificence about the way he plays. I thought we should give it as much help as we could, so I orchestrated the 'Marseillaise' around his trumpet playing. It is a wonderful moment because he's not a good player, and yet in the eyes of our Eric he's just fantastic. And then you see this cutaway of these kids, all of whom dream of only one thing at night and that's ending up being Wayne Rooney, or Berbatov, and it's just magical, him playing the trumpet for them while they play football.

The music behind the montages of Cantona's greatest goals is kind of my anthem for Eric. It's a very simple piano tune – just two shifting chords and then it modulates up. It was the first thing I wrote. I was sitting there thinking what a great job this is, I just played this thing and Ken said, 'Oh, I like that,' so that was that. It's a weird thing football – the way it can make your heart soar.

Sarah Ryan

Costume Designer

Ken and I talked about Eric Bishop, about what his life was like and his current mental state. We looked at photographs of the locations to get an idea of his background. Obviously Eric didn't have much money and his house is a bit of a mess, so you just know that his life is quite run down and his clothing will be quite run down too.

Obviously we needed a fair few Man U shirts. I actually threw in some old ones because Eric and his postmen have been fans for so long. Whether you notice it on screen I don't know because they are often underneath his clothing. When he takes off a layer you might get a flash of another shirt. He has several different ones. There was one he wore under his uniform a lot from the late eighties.

His daughter wears the one with the laced-up neck from the early 90s in the scene on the bus. Eric also has that one on when he's training with Big Eric. Then there's another one made of blue cotton that's an old fifties away strip. They're nice – I prefer them to be honest.

As the film goes on, as Eric's mental state improves, that's reflected in his dress but it's quite subtle. When he meets Lily he makes a little bit of an effort. He's put on a shirt. He starts off in a postal uniform that's really scruffy and then a few days later it's a better blue colour and slightly pressed. Nobody would know that but we ironed it and changed it from a grey blue to a better blue. And then we moved him on from there so even when he's dressed casually he's starting to think, 'I need to look a bit better' – he's thinking about himself in a way he wasn't before.

When it came to Eric Cantona, that was a bit of a thing. Initially, we were saying that because he just appears, is he appearing from the past, is he a ghost, is he the king? In my head I thought he could be dressed in a white suit or as this mad regal character. Ken was like, 'No, he's just like he is as he is now.' I'd got all excited but when you read the script it makes sense. So we tried to make him nondescript, in all these dark colours, even when he's training. Ken was just happy that he was who he was.

Football and Film
Paul Laverty

What about the idea of mixing film with football?

Has there ever been a more embarrassing moment in film history than Sly Stallone's cheetah-like performance as goalkeeper in *Escape to Victory*? It's so bad, it's brilliant. Anyone who tries to capture the excitement of an actual game in fiction just doesn't get it. What football fan can forget Steve McMahon, the Liverpool midfielder, holding up a finger to indicate just one minute left to go. (Last game of season 1989, in which Arsenal had to win by two goals.) In the dying seconds of the entire season Michael Thomas ran through from midfield to score and beat Liverpool 2-0. Arsenal became the new champions. Kenny Dalglish stares out in shock. Even now replaying the goal on YouTube almost twenty years later you can almost feel a collective effort from the Kop's entire subconscious willing Thomas into a headlong trip – but it never works – the goal is scored again, and the pain in the pit of the stomach will never go for those supporters.

But that is mild compared to Bayern Munich's trauma against Manchester United in the European cup final of '99; that inconsolable mountain of a centre back for Bayern, Samuel Kuffour, pounding the earth with his fists at the cosmic injustice of it all when they lose two goals in extra time after leading for the whole match. Or Ole Gunnar Solskjaer's ecstasy after scoring the winner. How can fictional managers compete with the charisma of Shankly or complexity of Ferguson? So we don't try to compete with the game itself, but ask why it is important in some people's lives.

I'll never forget once walking back to the centre of Glasgow from Parkhead after a Celtic victory. It was a freezing February more than twenty-five years ago and I have an image of this young lad soaked through, shivering, but with the biggest smile on his face. We got talking. 'It's brilliant man...for ninety minutes you get to forget all the rest of the shite in your life...' I wasn't writing then but often wondered what his life was like, so maybe this anonymous figure helped me too.

Why the scene with FC United?
There is an exchange in the script between Meatballs and Spleen as they drink with a mixture of Man U fans and those of FC United. Meatballs reflects on football fat cats. 'Daylight robbery...they went right into our Saturday afternoon and ripped our hearts out...then into our living rooms and stole our game!' Spleen: '...and here you are on Monday night disgracing yourselves to keep that fucker Murdoch happy.' Of course, poor old Spleen is desperate to see the game too, even on a Monday, on Murdoch's channel. The mind is willing, but the flesh is weak.

Author David Conn [*The Football Business*] is eloquent in his analysis of how big money, TV deals, and changing rules have affected our game. The postmen and many life-long supporters have been priced out, so the match on TV in a pub has become the option for many. It's a deep culture change. What is disgraceful too is how many chairmen and directors have made private fortunes from their so-called stewardship of the clubs, or should I say manipulation of loyalty. If I remember correctly the Hall family in Newcastle made up to 100 million and Alan Sugar made around 50 million. Edwards at United made a killing too.

FC United – ex-fans from United (and many still have very strong emotional links to Man U) set up their own club after United was taken over by the Glazers. I still find it stunning that this magnificent club with such a special history can be loaded with debt to allow these new US owners, with no previous connection to United, to buy it. I hope it doesn't end in tragedy. Football isn't just a commodity. Mere speculation on my part but I can only imagine this must have been a bitter pill for Alex Ferguson to swallow, a man for whom I have great personal respect. I'll always remember his loyalty to Cantona in his moments of crisis. FC United are determined that the new club, though modest, will be owned by the supporters. One member, one vote, no matter how much money they have or contribute. No masters. They are doing terrific things in their community too at a grassroots level. Ordinary parents can afford to bring their children once again. I was really impressed by them. I went to see them play. They got beat 3-2 that day but there was a marvelous noisy atmosphere and to my amazement they were still singing songs about Cantona.

I would like to thank all those who gave their support and expertise which helped me write this screenplay. In particular I would like to thank Colin Fraser, Juan Butragueño, Westley Eckhardt, Hearing Voices Network, Kathleen Conroy, Dr Theodor Mutale, Ron Coleman, Eileen Boyes, Mark Cohen, Alison Cohen, Tim Thomas, Pushy Khaneka, Dave Musker, Maruchi Delgado, Andy Walsh, Adam Brown, David Conn and Icíar Bollaín. A very special thanks to Kate Hughes for the idea of the Picasso postcard, and much more. Without the exceptional insight and generosity of Steve Sklair this story would not have been the same.

Paul Laverty has written the screenplays for seven previous full length feature films directed by Ken Loach: *Carla's Song* (1996), *My Name is Joe* (1998), *Bread and Roses* (2000), *Sweet Sixteen* (2002) – winner of Best Original Screenplay at Cannes – *Ae Fond Kiss* (2004), *The Wind That Shakes the Barley* (2006) – winner of the Palme d'Or at Cannes – and *It's A Free World* (2007) – winner of Best Original Screenplay at Venice Film Festival.

Film Credits

It all began with a beautiful pass from Eric Cantona...

Director	Ken Loach
Producer	Rebecca O'Brien
Screenplay	Paul Laverty
Executive Producers	Eric Cantona
	Pascal Caucheteux
	Vincent Maraval
Music	George Fenton
Editor	Jonathan Morris
Line Producer	Tim Cole
Costume Designer	Sarah Ryan
Sound Editor	Kevin Brazier
Locations	Emma Woodcock
Assistant Directors	David Gilchrist
	Michael Queen
Casting	Kahleen Crawford
Recordist	Ray Beckett
Photography	Barry Ackroyd
Production Designer	Fergus Clegg

Financials:

Canto Bros. Productions, Sixteen Films, Why Not Productions

Wild Bunch, Film4, Icon Film Distribution, North West Vision Media, France 2 Cinéma, Canal +, Ciné Cinéma, France 2, Sofica UGC 1, Diaphana Distribution, RTBF (Télévision belge), BIM Distribuzione, Les Films du Fleuve, La Région Wallonne, Cinéart, Tornasol Films, Alta Producción

Eric Bishop	Steve Evets
Eric Cantona	Lui-même
Lily	Stephanie Bishop
Ryan	Gerard Kearns
Jess	Stefan Gumbs
Sam	Lucy-Jo Hudson
Daisy	Cole and Dylan Williams
Young Eric	Matthew McNulty
Young Lily	Laura Ainsworth
Eric's Father	Maxton Beesley
Ryan's Girlfriend	Kelly Bowland
Nurse	Julie Brown
Meatballs	John Henshaw
Spleen	Justin Moorhouse
Jack	Des Sharples
Monk	Greg Cook
Judge	Mick Ferry
Smug	Smug Roberts
Travis	Johnny Travis
Zac	Steve Marsh
Buzz	Cleveland Campbell
Fenner	Ryan Pope

The Emperors of Rhythm

Omar Abdul, Adam Beresford, Ciaran Clancy, Steve Cook, Sheila Diamond, Marvin Gilbert, Ben Jackson, Wendy Kennedy, Trevor Dwyer Lynch, Jake Manning, Tom Meredith, Eddie Riley, Conor Saunders, Venn Tracey and Guy Wills

Stunt Co-ordinator	Paul Heasman
Stunt Performers	Stephanie Carey, Stuart Clark, Eunice Huthart, Derek Lea, Lee Sheward, Séon Rogers, Rocky Taylor
Production Co-ordinator	Eimhear McMahon
Production	Sean Jackson, Ella Brookes, Kate Cooper
3rd Assistant Director	Julie Heskin
Runner	Alistair Ramsden
Assistants	Jenny Anyon, Chris Cavanagh
Drivers	Chris Roden, Ian Percival, Jim Taylor, Johnny Mellor, David Walker
Unit Manager	Faye Newton
Location Scouts	Andy Ferrans, David Colenutt, Catherine Cooper
Focus Puller	Carl Hudson
Clapper Loaders	Amaury Duquenne, Joachim Philippe
Camera Trainee	Chris Wanklyn
2nd Unit Focus Puller	Olly Driscoll
Daily Technicians	Ben Appleton, Dave Ashby, Craig Mellor, Marc Tempest, Billy Tracey
Script Consultant	Roger Smith

Script Supervisor	Susanna Lenton
Stills Photographer	Joss Barratt
Advisors	Adam Brown,
	Bruce Devenport
Choreographer	Jude Goodier
Gaffer	Matthew Moffatt
Best Boy	Antoine Doyen
Electrician	Laurent Van Eijs
Boom Operator	Pete Murphy
Sound Assistant	Ben Collinson
Art Director	Julie Ann Horan
Assistant Art Director	Nic Henderson
Prop Buyer	Anita Gupta
Prop Master	Colin Mutch
Props	Mark Reynolds,
	Anthony Rutter,
	Simon Price
Armourers	Mark Shelley, Phil Stone
Action Vehicle Co-ordinator	Neil Adams
Dog Handler	Sonia Hooper
T.V. Operator	Dave Loveridge
Construction Manager	Danny Sumsion
Carpenters	David Richmond,
	Mark Brady, Tony Morris
Painters	Paul Curren, Bobby Gee,
	Jason Ragg, Martin Feely
Make-up and Hair Designer	Carli Mathers
Costume Supervisor	Rachel Selby

Costume Assistants	Nicky Baran, Lindsey Davidson
Dailies	Faye Aydin, Clair Blackmoore, Adelle Firth, Rowena Dean, Kim Freeland, Emma Vickers, Debbie Goodship, Abby Graves, Debs Hudson, Mairi Morrison, Matt Price, Spob
Production Accountant	Tina Shadick
Assistant Accountant	Habib Rahman
Auditor	Malde & Company
1st Assistant Editor	Anthony Morris
2nd Assistant Editor	Paul Clegg
Sound Transfers	Steve Carr
Sound Editors	Robert Brazier, Ben Brazier
Foley Artists	Rowena Wilkinson, Sue Harding
Re-recording Mixers	Ian Tapp, James Doyle
Paramedic	Dave Nicholas
Caterers	Michael Ross, Red Chutney
Security	Billy Robinson, Capricorn Security
Rushes	Alistair Murray, Gary Preston

Music Recorded by	Steve Price at
	Angel Recording Studios
Pro Tools	Mat Bartram
Music Associate	Simon Chamberlain
Musicians' Contractor	Isobel Griffiths

Musicians	
Solo Bass	Chris Laurence
Piano	Simon Chamberlain
Guitar	John Parricelli
Bass Guitar	Steve Pearce
Percussion	Frank Ricotti
Drums	Neal Wilkinson,
	Ralph Salmins
Trumpet	Eric Cantona,
	Mike Lovatt
Leader / 1st Viola	Peter Lale

Original Soundtrack available on Debonair

Songs

'Out of Dreams' performed by The Rascals, written by Miles Kane & Joe Edwards, published by Deltasonic Music Limited

'Lily the Pink' written by Trad/Gorman/McGear/McGough, published by Noel Gay Music Co Limited

'High School Confidential' written by Jerry Lee Lewis & Ron Hargrave, published by Carlin Music Corp

'It's Late' written by Dorsey Burnette, published by Sony/ATV and EMI UnitedPartnership Ltd

'Blue Suede Shoes' performed by Elvis Presley, (P)1956 Sony Music Entertainment Inc. Licensed courtesy of Sony Music Entertainment UK Limited

'Ready For War' written and performed by Marvin 'Crown Jewelz' Gilbert & Omar 'Mister O' Abdul, produced by Andrew 'Kings Club' Malley

Football Archive
The Premier League Archive
The Football Association
Commentary material supplied by the ITV Sport Archive

'The Descent' courtesy of Celador Films Limited. All rights reserved.

'The Cottage' courtesy of Sony Pictures Home Entertainment Inc.

Picasso Pablo, Blue Dove © Succession Picasso / DACS 2008

With thanks to:
Stevie Sklair; Philip Townsend, Alex Remington, Manchester United Football Club; Paul McKenna; Vinny Thompson and Andy Walsh, FC United; David Conn; Juan Butragueño; Westley Eckhardt; Hearing Voices Network; Kathleen Conroy; Dr. Theodor Mutale; Ron Coleman; Supt. Dave Musker; Eileen Boyes; Colin Fraser; Tim Thomas; Mark Cohen; Alison Cohen; Danny Jackson; Brigitte Maccioni, Pierre Héros, Bertrand Hassini-Bonnette, Laurent Hassid, Michel Saint-Jean, Anne Mathieu, Anne Flamant, Cédric Plantier; Let's Go Global; Lancashire County Highways; Hughie at Trafford General Hospital; Swinton Palais; SW Manchester Cricket Club;

Manchester Metropolitan; Salford Museum and Gallery; Millhouse Developments; Barry Sharples; Ali Sadegholnegat; Martin & Co; and the residents of Keppel Road and Chatsworth Road, Manchester

Lawyers	Stephen Grosz,
	Bindman & Partners;
	John Lafferty;
	Christian Valsamidis
	& Emmanuelle Bergeret,
	Taylor Wessing
Insurance	Media Insurance Brokers
For Why Not Productions	Georges Bereta,
	Lucie Borleteau,
	David Frenkel
For Wild Bunch	Marie Besançon
For Canto Bros	Jean Marie Cantona,
	Joel Cantona
For Les Films du Fleuve	Olivier Bronckart,
	Delphine Tomson,
	Tania Antonioli
For Film4	Tessa Ross, Peter Carlton,
	Paul Grindey
For RTBF (Belgian Television)	Arlette Zylberberg,
	Frédérique Larmagnac,
	Catherine Poels

Financing

Casa Kafka Pictures (Isabelle Molhant), Inver Invest (Muriel Bostyn), Petroliper, P. Lemmens Air Movement Company, Wilmet, Petromeuse Services, Vandekerckove, RMA

Avec le soutien de la Région Wallonne, du Centre du Cinéma

et de l'Audiovisuel de la Communauté Française de Belgique et des Télédistributeurs Wallons, et du Tax Shelter du Gouvernement Belge

Titles	Martin Bullard, JCA
Titles Design	Martin Butterworth, Creative Partnership
Laboratory	Color by Deluxe
Neg Cutters	Cutting Edge
Film Stock	Fujifilm
Camera and Lights	Eye Lite Group
Cutting Rooms	Goldcrest
Sound Re-recording	Pinewood Studios
Publicity	Charles McDonald
International Sales	Wild Bunch

A British/French/Italian/Belgian/Spanish Co-Production
Filmed on location in Manchester

The characters and incidents portrayed and the names used herein are fictitious, and any similarity to any name or incident, or the character or biography of any person, is purely coincidental and unintentional.

MPAA No. 44702

© Canto Brothers SA, Sixteen Films Ltd, Why Not Productions SA, Wild Bunch SA, Channel Four Television Corporation, France 2 Cinéma, BIM Distribuzione, Les Films du Fleuve, RTBF (Belgian Television), Tornasol Films

MMIX

Photo Captions

Production Stills

1. Young Eric (Matthew McNulty) and Young Lily (Laura Ainsworth)
2. Young Eric (Matthew McNulty) and Young Lily (Laura Ainsworth) dancing to the Emperors of Rhythm
3. Young Eric (Matthew McNulty) and his father (Maxton Beesley) at Sam's christening
4. Young Eric (Matthew McNulty)
5. Lily (Stephanie Bishop) waits for Eric with Daisy
6. Eric Bishop (Steve Evets)
7. Eric Bishop (Steve Evets)
8. Eric Bishop (Steve Evets) lets off some steam
9. Sam (Lucy-Jo Hudson) and her father Eric (Steve Evets)
10. Supporters bus en route to the game
11. (l-r) Smug (Smug Roberts), Meatballs (John Henshaw) and Monk (Greg Cook) discuss getting Eric back on track
12. Meatballs (John Henshaw) thinks he has the answer to it all
13. Meatballs (John Henshaw) begins the meditation sessions
14. (l-r) Jack (Des Sharples) and Eric (Steve Evets) take part in some light meditation
15. Eric Bishop (Steve Evets) with his hero
16. Eric Cantona
17. Spleen (Justin Moorhouse)
18. Match day at the pub: Spleen (Justin Moorhouse) gets over excited
19. Eric Cantona and Eric Bishop (Steve Evets)
20. Eric Bishop (Steve Evets) and Eric Cantona
21. (r-l) Eric (Steve Evets) confronts Ryan (Gerard Kearns) about the gun in the house
22. Zac (Steve Marsh)
23. (l-r) Buzz (Cleveland Campbell) and Fenner (Ryan Pope) use their dog to terrorise Eric
24. Jess (Stefan Gumbs)
25. Eric Bishop (Steve Evets)
26. Eric (Steve Evets), Monk (Greg Cook) and The Judge (Mick Ferry) and the other postmen formulate a plan of action
27. (l-r) The Judge (Mick Ferry), Travis (Johnny Travis), Meatballs (John Henshaw), Jack (Des Sharples), Eric (Steve Evets), Smug (Smug Roberts), Monk (Greg Cook) and Spleen (Justin Moorhouse)

28. Eric Cantona

29. The Cantonas arrive to teach Zac a lesson

30. Ryan (Gerard Kearns), Meatballs (John Henshaw) and Eric (Steve Evets) take on Zac's dog

31. Zac (Steve Marsh) gets taught a lesson

32. Eric Cantona

33. Monk (Greg Cook), The Judge (Mick Ferry), Travis (Johnny Travis), Jess (Stefan Gumbs), Lily (Stephanie Bishop), Jack (Des Sharples), Sam (Lucy-Jo Hudson), Spleen (Justin Moorhouse), Eric (Steve Evets), Ryan (Gerard Kearns) and Smug (Smug Robert) celebrate Sam's graduation

34. Eric (Steve Evets) and Lily (Stephanie Bishop) pose for a photo at Sam's graduation

Behind the Scenes Stills

35. Ken Loach and Eric Cantona

36. Ken Loach and Paul Laverty

37. Ken Loach

38. Producer, Rebecca O'Brien

39. Ken Loach with focus puller, Carl Hudson

40. (l-r) Stephanie Bishop (Lily), Ken Loach and Steve Evets (Eric)

41. Stephanie Bishop (Lily) and Steve Evets (Eric)

42. Matthew McNulty (Young Eric) and Steve Evets (Eric)

43. Steve Evets (Eric)

44. Ken Loach talks with Eric Cantona while Steve Evets (Eric) warms up in the background

45. (l-r) Justin Moorhouse (Spleen), Des Sharples (Jack), Eric Cantona, Steve Evets (Eric) and John Henshaw (Meatballs)

46. (l-r) Ken Loach, Johnny Travis (Travis), Mick Ferry (The Judge) and Smug Roberts (Smug)

47. Prop boys, Colin Mutch and Mark Reynolds, touch up the Cantona masks

48. Justin Moorhouse (Spleen)

49. Ken Loach coordinates the Cantonas

50. Eric Cantona with FC Utd fans

51. Barry Ackroyd (DOP)

52. Recordist, Ray Beckett

53. The camera department with (r-l) production designer, Fergus Clegg and Barry Ackroyd

54. Paul Laverty looks for mischief

© Photographs: Joss Barratt

For further information on this book,
and other titles from Route please visit:

www.route-online.com